MORE PRAISE FOR *Making A Difference II: More Tips, Ideas and Stories to Change Your World*

"Keep this book by your night table. When you wake up in the morning, you will be ready with all the many ways in which you can make a difference. Lisa Dietlin has assembled clever, insightful and often humorous tips on how to make a difference in the world every day. The tips make us realize that it is the small things that often make a difference. And, in the words of Anne Frank, 'How wonderful it is that nobody need wait a single moment before starting to improve the world.'"

Maria Wynne
Chief Executive Officer
Girl Scouts of Greater Chicago and Northwest Indiana

"Lisa Dietlin is a force. Lisa reminds us all that giving not only rewards the giver and makes a fuller life, it is fun! To know Lisa is to become immersed in a sea of positive thought, backed by practical knowledge, and powered by a tenacious will to spread her philanthropic message. *Making a Difference II* is a great way to start the day. This book will help the reader forget their own troubles and get on to the business of helping others, which is the finest path to happiness."

Matthew L. Jimenez, MD
Illinois Bone and Joint Institute
Clinical Associate Professor
Department Orthopaedic Surgery, University of Illinois

"Anyone can generalize about making a difference. Far better is how Lisa Dietlin gives us a specific way to lift up our world for every day of the year, and thereby lift up ourselves. From the bold strokes of the famous to the small graces of the nameless, her examples call me to realize, 'I could do that. I should do that, and I will.'"

Dr. Olin Joynton, PhD
President
Alpena Community College

P9-EJZ-245

"We should all seek to make a difference. Lisa M Dietlin knows how we can. This book is a treasure chest of thoughtful ways we can make the most of our talents, time and money. "

H. Art Taylor
President and CEO
BBB Wise Giving Alliance

"Once again, Dietlin shows us that the simplest act can be the catalyst for change in our communities and in ourselves."

Vicki Escarra
President and CEO
Feeding America

"This book proves there are no excuses and no limits to making a difference. Ms. Dietlin has compiled an amazing source of inspiration and motivation. I plan to use this both personally and professionally."

Robert Mendonsa
Chief Executive Office
Aetna Better Health, Illinois

Courageous
Dreams
PUBLISHING HOUSE
PO Box 4781 • Chicago, IL • 60680 • 773.772.2402

Book Design by Katie Nordt

Making a Difference II

More Tips, Ideas and Stories to Change Your World

Lisa M. Dietlin

Here's to always making a difference in the world!

Dedication

To the Members of the Class of 1981

During my youth and childhood, I attended three schools. Recently I have reconnected with many classmates from all of them. This reconnection reminds me on a daily basis that everyone you encounter makes a difference in your life!

This book is dedicated to the classmates from —

Alpena High School — The Wildcats [Alpena, MI]

Park High School — The Rangers [Livingston, MT]

Hill-McCloy HighSchool — The Rams [Montrose, MI]

I will always remember and cherish the friendships!

You all have made a difference in my life!

Acknowledgments

This book is my third and I am just as excited about its publication as I was the first and second books I wrote. What I have realized more and more during this book writing process is that the old saying is really true, "...it truly does take a village" to write a book.

As you might suspect, there are many, many people to thank for their contributions to the writing process.

First, thank you to everyone who works or tries every day to make a difference. You truly inspire me on a daily basis!

Second, thank you to those who submitted ideas for this book; I enjoyed reading your stories, tips and ideas and encourage everyone to keep sharing with me how they make a difference or what they have witnessed.

Thanks must go to the clients my company, Lisa M. Dietlin and Associates, Inc. (LMDA), serves. The work you are doing is truly amazing and at times, life altering or life saving. Your work is the catalyst for transformation in the world to happen and for that I am privileged to play a small role in your work.

The LMDA staff bears the brunt of the issues and work that arise when I am writing a book and for their efforts as well as their constant support, I am eternally grateful. Thanks should go to Julie Fregetto, Nadine Donajkowski, Barbara Figgins, Jeri Frederickson, Kristina Butler, Amy Murdoch, Bianca Andinc and Liz Abello. Because of the work you do, I was able to finish this book on time! You made a difference!

A number of friends as well as colleagues became constant sources of information and provided "tips" for this book. Thanks go to Renee Torina, Nadine Donajkowski, Chuck Hein, Dr. Bob Deaver, Mary Ann

Beckwith, Evelyn Ward, Stacy French Reynolds, Evelyn Ward, Stacy French Reynolds, Ann Brinkman Carstensen, Kim Klee and others. Your willingness to be on the hunt for stories and tips for this book truly did make a difference!

To many of my friends who offered a kind word or supportive email as I was writing this book, I am grateful. Thanks goes to Margaret Soffin, Valerie Ingram, Janet Katowitz, Kathryn Tack, Julia Koch, Suzanne Jurva, Karen Hynes, Sandra Mattison, Aimee Daniels, Annette Lozon, Caroline Coppola, Leticia Herrera, Cathy Cheshire Shook, Cibeline Sariano, Marlie Sailer, Erin Minne', Kurt Hill, Jodie LaRoche, Jenny Porter Carrillo, Marcy Simpson Euler, Ken Lampar, Jim Mitchell and Lisa Guzman. Your friendship and support makes a huge difference in my life!

To me, life is a grand adventure! Often I find people are so scared of failing at the adventure that at times they are not willing to even try or start something new. This year commit to taking chances and embracing risks...this is one way great change can occur and make the difference you seek!

Finally, courage is the virtue I embrace the most...to the readers of this book, I hope you find courage daily to try to make a difference in your community and world. I encourage you to realize that your efforts, whether big or small, do cause change to happen!

Ask yourself this question daily, are you M.A.D. (Making A Difference)?

Lisa M. Dietlin
NOVEMBER 2011

"$\mathcal{A}$re you $\mathcal{MAD}$ (Making A Difference)? Four
(4) Recommended Steps For How To Use This Book"

$\mathcal{S}$tep 1: Read a tip every day

$\mathcal{S}$tep 2: Try to implement the suggestion or use it as
motivation to try to make a difference on a daily basis

$\mathcal{S}$tep 3: Write down your reaction to the tip and/or what
you did to try to make a difference

$\mathcal{S}$tep 4: Submit your stories to MAD@lmdietlin.com
[they could be included in the next edition of this book]

Making a Difference

What are you thankful for? What person or organization has made a difference in your life? Take a moment today to reflect and then offer up a thank you! If you have time, consider contacting that person or organization to let them know their efforts did make a difference!

_____

_____

_____

_____

_____

_____

_____

_____

_____

_____

_____

_____

_____

_____

_____

_____

_____

_____

_____

_____

_____

_____

Making a Difference

Paul Newman, the actor, reportedly initially rejected the idea of Newman's Own saying, "Are you crazy? Put my face on the label of salad dressing?" He then got the idea believing why not go to the fullest and the silliest lengths in exploiting oneself giving the proceeds back to the community? He did this and made a difference with more than $290 million being donated to charity!

Making a Difference

During tough economic times, many people struggle to make ends meet. They often become stressed thinking about what gifts they can purchase and give for birthdays, weddings and holidays. What about a gift of service? Offer to clean someone's house, provide childcare, plant flowers, wash their car, drive them someplace, care for their pets when they are gone...the list goes on and on of ways you can make a difference without spending a dime!

Making a Difference

On a flight, I was reading the airline magazine and learned about Soldiers' Angels, a group providing comfort to soldiers (soldiersangels.org). In visiting the website I learned there are over 1000 soldiers waiting for "adoption" by volunteers. Volunteers send care packages, letters, laptops, flights, etc. Check it out; the opportunities to be supportive and make a difference are endless.

Making a Difference

Once a day, do something to make a difference. Make this your daily goal. It will be like throwing a stone in a pond with many ripples flowing outwards from the center of your act. You will be making a difference!

Making a Difference

In my hometown (Alpena, Michigan), Elly and John own a maple syrup farm. In touring the "Sugar Shack" of the Diamond Rock Maple Farm I learned not only about how maple syrup is made, but also that this couple donates 100% of all the proceeds annually to charity! They keep none of the money made by selling pints and quarts of syrup but rather choose a charity or two annually and donate all the money! Talk about making a difference!

_____

_____

_____

_____

_____

_____

_____

_____

_____

_____

_____

_____

_____

_____

_____

_____

_____

Making a Difference

I live in a townhome association that has a lot of parents with young children. Recently, they let me in on a brilliant idea. It seems these parents were having difficulties affording babysitters and going out. The solution was they agreed to take turns watching each other's children as long as the children were already put to bed and it was after 7 pm. What a brilliant idea and a great way they are all making a difference!

Making a Difference

In 1938, the people in charge of the Palm Beach Invitational golf tournament started something extraordinary that eventually helped millions of people. They donated $10,000 from the tournament to local charities. Today, the PGA Tour has donated more than $1.5 billion to nonprofit organizations. Imagine if those few people in 1938 could see what they started and how they made a difference!

_____

_____

_____

_____

_____

_____

_____

_____

_____

_____

_____

_____

_____

_____

_____

_____

Making a Difference

Do you think before you print? Many of us automatically print everything that comes into our email inbox. Stop and think for a minute. Does the item you are viewing need to be printed or will an electronic version of it suffice? By thinking before you print, you will be making a difference!

Making a Difference

The celebration of the life of Dr. Martin Luther King Jr. (MLK) occurs in mid-January. Recently it has become a day dedicated to community service. Consider taking some time on the next MLK holiday to give back by finding a project or activity you can do either by yourself or with family and friends. By doing this you will be starting a new tradition and making a difference!

Making a Difference

What do John Arnold, Michael Bloomberg, Warren Buffet, the Fisher Family, Bill and Melinda Gates, Julian Robertson and Mark Zuckerberg have in common? According to Eli Broad they are philanthropists having an impact on the well-being of people around the world! Take time to learn about their efforts to change the world. It just might make a difference in how you view what you can do!

_____

_____

_____

_____

_____

_____

_____

_____

_____

_____

_____

_____

_____

_____

_____

_____

_____

_____

Making a Difference

Did you hear about the Canadian couple who won $11.2 million in the lottery? They shared that almost all of the money would be directed to taking care of family members, then the rest would be donated to various organizations and institutions instead of spending it on themselves. Yes, they are giving it away! Talk about making a difference! Would you give money to charity if you won the lottery?

_____

_____

_____

_____

_____

_____

_____

_____

_____

_____

_____

_____

_____

_____

_____

_____

_____

_____

_____

Making a Difference

Do you stop at roadside historical markers? Many of them tell the stories of people or groups of people who because of their actions changed things. Make it a point to stop at roadside historical markers to learn about these people and what they did to make a difference!

_____

_____

_____

_____

_____

_____

_____

_____

_____

_____

_____

_____

_____

_____

_____

_____

_____

_____

_____

Making a Difference

In 2011, *MarketWatch* had an article stating Americans are again in a giving mood! This is good news as charitable donations are up. While most of us will receive multiple requests, usually via our mailbox, I recommend not letting let guilt drive your charitable decisions. Make a plan, set a budget then make your donation! Every dollar counts, and you will be making a difference!

Making a Difference

Are you always looking for a last minute gift? Financial advisor and author Suze Orman has a book titled, *Thoughts That Can Change Your Life*. What is unique about this book is that she donates all her royalties to the Avon Foundation for Women. Consider purchasing this book as a gift for many on your list! You will be making a difference in at least two ways!

Making a Difference

My best friend Mary Ann told me she received a call from her granddaughter Kylee. Kylee had become aware there were poor kids in the world that did not have books to read. She asked her grandmother to send her money because her goal was to raise $50 to buy books through her school. She even talked her grandmother into doubling her pledge! If a seven year old child can make a difference, what can you do?

_____

_____

_____

_____

_____

_____

_____

_____

_____

_____

_____

_____

_____

_____

_____

_____

George Bernard Shaw, the Irish playwright, said, "People are always blaming circumstances for what they are. I don't believe in circumstances. The people who get on in this world are the people who get up and look for the circumstances they want, and, if they can't find them, make them." What can you do today to embrace or change your circumstances in order to make a difference?

_____

_____

_____

_____

_____

_____

_____

_____

_____

_____

_____

_____

_____

_____

_____

_____

_____

Making a Difference

Have you heard about the Shoestring Philanthropist? For more than 22 years, Marc Gold has been transforming lives in Asia by giving away money from 50 cents to $500, with it on average being $5. It is estimated he has changed about 50,000 lives! Could you be a shoestring philanthropist? What could you do with your loose change or dollar bills that would change someone's life and make a difference?

_____

_____

_____

_____

_____

_____

_____

_____

_____

_____

_____

_____

_____

_____

_____

_____

_____

_____

Making a Difference

In this day and age, it is easy to get overwhelmed and lose focus. Dr. Stephen Post shares that an attitude of gratitude can change your life. He says to focus on things for which you are grateful for 15 minutes a day and you will significantly increase your body's natural antibodies. Spend time today thinking about for what you are most grateful. It will make a difference!

_____

_____

_____

_____

_____

_____

_____

_____

_____

_____

_____

_____

_____

_____

_____

_____

_____

_____

_____

Making a Difference

I read an article that discussed American wine producers naming their wines with letters. One vineyard located in the state of Washington named its 2007 Columbia Valley Red Wine "O" for opportunity and gives part of the proceeds from the sale of each bottle to a scholarship fund for underprivileged youth. Consider purchasing products that have a charitable component. You will be making a difference!

Making a Difference

Robert Frost, the great American poet, wrote, "Two roads diverged in a wood, and I – I took the one less traveled by, and that has made all the difference." Take the road less traveled for the next year and see how it makes a difference!

_____

_____

_____

_____

_____

_____

_____

_____

_____

_____

_____

_____

_____

_____

_____

_____

_____

_____

_____

_____

_____

Making a Difference

Most of us have heard of Anne Frank, the young girl whose diary became an international bestseller after her death in the German concentration camp. I found this quote from her that I think is perfect for today's word. "How wonderful it is that nobody need wait a single moment before starting to improve the world." Think about this statement and start today to make a difference in your world!

_____

_____

_____

_____

_____

_____

_____

_____

_____

_____

_____

_____

_____

_____

_____

_____

_____

_____

Making a Difference

I came across this quote and love it! The author is unknown, but the message is worth remembering, "Go the extra mile. It's never crowded." This statement is very true! Do something today to help someone or change a situation. Go that extra mile. You might be alone on the path but you will be making a difference!

Making a Difference

According to a *USA Today* article, nonprofits are relying more on volunteers due to budget cuts. Organizations such as food pantries, volunteer fire departments and others providing much needed services are in need of help. Whether working or not, consider carving out some time in your week to volunteer to help your community during these tough economic times. You will be making a difference!

Making a Difference

TIP OF THE DAY

Bullying and bullies come in all sizes, shapes and forms. The types of bullying range from physical to cyber to verbal – the list goes on and on. Can you recognize the warning signs of someone being bullied? Do your part today to know the signs of bullying and then work to intervene and change situations. By coming together around this issue we can make a difference!

Making a Difference

American psychologist and philosopher William James is quoted as saying, "Act as if what you do makes a difference. It does." Think about that statement today as you go about your daily routine. Pay attention to what you do and how it makes a difference!

Making a Difference

Dr. Seuss, the famed children's author, said, "Unless someone like you cares a whole awful lot, nothing is going to get better. It's not." A simple statement that is so true. You need to care and be willing to step outside your comfort zone sometimes to make a difference!

Making a Difference

It has been 150 years since the Civil War began in the United States. I learned that Civil War sites are disappearing at the rate of an acre an hour! You can help! To learn more about what happened 150 years ago go to the website (give150.com) whose message and effort is to "Preserve Our Past. Protect Our Future". Your support and donations will benefit the Civil War Preservation Trust and the National Park Foundation. You can make a difference!

Making a Difference

John F. Kennedy, the 35th President of the United States, said, "Children are the world's most valuable resource and its best hope for the future." How true! Pay attention to the children in your life. Your actions and interactions do make a difference!

_____

_____

_____

_____

_____

_____

_____

_____

_____

_____

_____

_____

_____

_____

_____

_____

_____

_____

_____

Making a Difference

I attended the opening of the Wounded Warrior Art Exhibit in Chicago. What an amazing show Sponsored by the American Academy of Orthopaedic Surgeons, it's an exhibit of art by medical professionals from their experiences of treating our injured military personnel! Check it out (woundedinactionart.org); see how medical doctors, nurses and others are making a difference in so many ways!

Making a Difference

Famed scientist Albert Einstein said, "There are two ways to live your life. One is as though nothing is a miracle. The other is as though everything is a miracle." Everything you experience and do can be a miracle and can make a difference!

_____

_____

_____

_____

_____

_____

_____

_____

_____

_____

_____

_____

_____

_____

_____

_____

_____

_____

_____

_____

_____

Making a Difference

An unknown person said or wrote these words and how true they are, "Being good is commendable, but only when it is combined with doing good is it useful." When we teach and tell our children to be good, let's also remember to tell them to do good. Lead by example. You will be making a difference!

_____

_____

_____

_____

_____

_____

_____

_____

_____

_____

_____

_____

_____

_____

_____

_____

_____

_____

Making a Difference

The great physician Albert Schweitzer said, "Wherever a man turns he can find someone who needs him." Think about who needs you today and how you can make a difference. It's the only thing that really matters.

Making a Difference

Most of us have heard the Biblical story of the Good Samaritan. Martin Luther King, Jr. summed up the story by saying this, "The first question which the priest and the Levite asked was, "If I stop to help this man, what will happen to me?" But...the Good Samaritan reversed the question, "If I do not stop to help this man, what will happen to him?" Which question do you ask and how does it make a difference?

_____

_____

_____

_____

_____

_____

_____

_____

_____

_____

_____

_____

_____

_____

_____

_____

_____

Making a Difference

I came across this quote and fell in love with it. While its author is unknown, its message is a good reminder to us. It states, "Those who can, do. Those who can do more, volunteer." Who are you and what can you do to make a difference?

_____

_____

_____

_____

_____

_____

_____

_____

_____

_____

_____

_____

_____

_____

_____

_____

_____

_____

_____

Making a Difference

There is a saying from Buddha that I like, "Thousands of candles can be lighted from a single candle, and the life of that candle will not be shortened." Translate this into doing good deeds for others. What can you do to make a difference? You can be assured that your candle will not be shortened by doing this.

_____

_____

_____

_____

_____

_____

_____

_____

_____

_____

_____

_____

_____

_____

_____

_____

_____

_____

Making a Difference

The American author and poet Henry David Thoreau is credited with saying, "Not only must we be good, but we must also be good for something." What are you good for and how can you use it to make a difference today?

Making a Difference

My friend, Evelyn, gave me a book titled, *One Simple Act* by Debbie Macomber. It is a wonderful work and an opportunity to discover the power of generosity. I highly recommend it! You will find hidden stories that will change your outlook and help you to continue making a difference through generous acts!

Making a Difference

We often hear that you reap what you sow; that what you give will come back tenfold. In Debbie Macomber's book, *One Simple Act*, she illustrates this point through the telling of the story of two young men working their way through college at Stanford University in 1892. Their funds were very low so they decided to hold a concert with the proceeds after costs being theirs for their bills. The manager of famous pianist Ignacy Jan Paderewski insisted on a guarantee of $2000, which they readily agreed to. As you probably suspect they did not raise the $2000 but only $1600 which they gave to the pianist after the concert. When he learned of the situation, he tore up the contract, told them to take their expenses out of the $1600 plus 10% each for their work and he kept the balance. Years later Paderewski became the Prime Minister of Poland. During a devastating war, the Polish people were starving and Paderewski needed to find food to feed his people. He turned to one man he knew could help him, President Herbert Hoover. Upon meeting Hoover to thank him for the food, he was surprised to hear the President say, "That's all right, Mr. Paderewski. Besides you don't remember it, but you helped me once when I was a student at college and I was in a hole." What a story! What a way two men unselfishly made a difference!

Making a Difference

The author Oscar Wilde is credited with saying, "The smallest act of kindness is worth more than the grandest intention." Many of us have the best of intentions, but what can we do, however small, that will really make a difference?

_____

_____

_____

_____

_____

_____

_____

_____

_____

_____

_____

_____

_____

_____

_____

_____

_____

_____

_____

_____

Making a Difference

The 32nd President of the United States, Franklin D. Roosevelt, said, "We cannot always build the future for our youth, but we can build our youth for the future." What are you doing today to insure the next generation is poised and ready to make a difference?

Making a Difference

Facebook, Twitter, LinkedIn and a host of websites allow us to be in constant contact with others. These technological advances bring home what the Herman Melville, author of *Moby Dick*, said more than 100 years ago, "We cannot live only for ourselves. A thousand fibers connect us with our fellow men." Remember, we are connected to each other and what you do does make a difference!

_____

_____

_____

_____

_____

_____

_____

_____

_____

_____

_____

_____

_____

_____

_____

_____

_____

_____

Making a Difference

Leo Buscaglia, author and motivational speaker, whose works and words are known to many throughout the world is credited with saying, "Too often we underestimate the power of a touch, a smile, a kind word, a listening ear, an honest compliment, or the smallest act of caring, all of which have the potential to turn a life around." Which of the above things could you do today that you now realize would make a difference in someone's life?

_____

_____

_____

_____

_____

_____

_____

_____

_____

_____

_____

_____

_____

_____

_____

_____

Making a Difference

In 2011, I attended the Grand Rapids Economics Club lunch to hear Lord Charles Spencer, Princess Diana's brother, speak about her charitable work. He explained how her efforts changed the way many viewed HIV/AIDS, leprosy, land mines, etc. Princess Diana was a humanitarian and a philanthropist. It is said when she married one billion people watched; when she died 2 ½ billion watched the funeral procession! Her efforts, work and life made a difference!

_____

_____

_____

_____

_____

_____

_____

_____

_____

_____

_____

_____

_____

_____

_____

_____

_____

_____

Making a Difference

The Diana Awards were established in 1999 shortly after Princess Diana's death. It is hoped the awards will reflect Princess Diana's commitment to helping and supporting young people. The award is given annually to inspirational young people. Those selected to receive the award are honored for their commitment to the school, family or community and do things such as peer mentor, fundraise, volunteer, etc. The Diana Awards are an effort to recognize young people for making a difference!!

Making a Difference

In 2010, Haiti was rocked by a devastating earthquake killing more than 230,000 people and uprooting lives. It is estimated that it will take ten years to rebuild and reconstruct the island. Much work needs to be done. While criticism has been voiced about the slow pace of recovery, improvements are happening. You can still help by making a financial donation, volunteering or simply offering up a prayer. All of these ideas can and do make a difference!

_____

_____

_____

_____

_____

_____

_____

_____

_____

_____

_____

_____

_____

_____

_____

_____

_____

_____

Making a Difference

Dr. Martin Luther King, Jr. said,

"Faith is taking the first step even when you don't see the entire staircase." Do you have faith to do something for someone else? To volunteer? To help a new nonprofit? Try today to make a difference by taking the first step!

Making a Difference

Many of us wonder what we can do to help our military men and women in the Army. Consider becoming active in a Family Readiness Group (FRG). FRGs are comprised of military leaders, family members, soldiers, civilian employees and volunteers. They provide support and enhance the flow of information. Activities vary depending on if it is taking place pre or post deployment. FRGs make a difference and you can, too!

Making a Difference

Have you heard of the Kyoto Prizes? Started by an ordained Buddhist priest, Dr. Inamori is both an entrepreneur and believer that life's greatest calling is to work for the greater good of humankind. In the 1980s, determined to give back, he started the Inamori Foundation and the Kyoto Prizes. The Kyoto Prizes honor men and women who make significant contributions to humanity of advanced technology, basic sciences as well as arts and philosophy. Thanks to Dr. Inamori for making a difference!

Making a Difference

Most of us know what the Super Bowl is...the championship game for the National Football League. Did you know it is also a volunteer opportunity? It is estimated that 10,000 volunteers are needed annually to make sure the Super Bowl goes off without a hitch. What a unique volunteer opportunity and a good way to make a difference!

Making a Difference

James Owen is an assistant professor at the University of Southern California who loves books! On a trip to Indonesia's East Java province, he was overwhelmed by the problems facing many people, including 10,000 who had been displaced because of mudslides. In 2009, he began asking for donations to build libraries in towns that had been devastated by the slides. In the first year, his organization built 22 libraries and established a mobile library, too. Thanks to James for making a difference to so many people!

Making a Difference

Most of us have heard about The Giving Pledge, the effort by Bill and Melinda Gates as well as Warren Buffet to convince billionaires to give away half their fortune during their lifetimes. They are having success. What most of us don't know is that this effort was done more than 100 years ago by John D. Rockefeller and Andrew Carnegie who encouraged other tycoons of their generation to give away their fortunes during their lifetime rather than leaving it all to their heirs. Following great examples is definitely a way to make a difference!

_____

_____

_____

_____

_____

_____

_____

_____

_____

_____

_____

_____

_____

_____

_____

Making a Difference

William Schambra, director of the Bradley Center for Philanthropy and Civic Renewal, says that the quest for discovering root causes of problems captures philanthropists in every generation. While this is good, it usually doesn't work. Finding that one thing that will make a difference in an area or problem is difficult. Instead work every day to make a difference with the problem you see in your immediate community or world!

Making a Difference

So Others Might Eat (some.org) is a nonprofit organization based in Washington, DC that has assisted the homeless and needy people for more than 40 years. They also treat the ill through their medical, dental and mental health programs as well as training people for jobs. As their website says, "They have helped thousands of people get off the streets, transform their lives and live independently." I would add they have also made a huge difference in lives of many!

Making a Difference

Research has been done that shows a daily gratitude exercise where individuals purposefully focus on specific things for which they are grateful result in positive states of alertness, enthusiasm, determination, energy and attentiveness! What could you be thankful for today that would make a difference in your life and the lives of others around you?

_____

_____

_____

_____

_____

_____

_____

_____

_____

_____

_____

_____

_____

_____

_____

_____

_____

_____

Making a Difference

The Boy Scouts of America is still a relevant organization for young boys. It is one of the largest nonprofit organizations in the country. For the past 100 years, the organization has worked to build future leaders of this country by combining educational activities and lifelong values with fun. Check out the Boy Scouts (scouting.org)! They are still making a difference!

Making a Difference

Listening is a great gift! In our society of constant noise, we often forget that sometimes the best thing we can do and ultimate gift we can give is to listen to our family and friends. Be purposeful and listen carefully today. What an easy way to make a difference!

Making a Difference

Most of us remember exactly where we were on 9/11. Many of us, in an instant, can recall the sights and images that flooded our television and computer screens in the hours and days that followed. I learned that during this time some parents wrote to Mr. Rogers, the much loved television personality, asking for advice of what to tell their children. Mr. Rogers told them to watch the helpers. This was great advice for both adults and children. He told parents to not focus on the pain and horror, but to focus on those who were rescuing, healing, comforting and rebuilding. He suggested sharing those powerful images with their children. What I remember most about 9/11 are the firefighters, both those from New York and those from around the country and world that came to help! I often think of the difference they made in the lives of so many!

Making a Difference

In 2011, Bowling Green State University (BGSU) announced a transformational gift. BGSU stated that for 60 years, Findlay native William (Bill) Frack had followed the BGSU men's basketball team. He then took steps to strengthen the program with a series of irrevocable trusts that have a combined value of more than $10 million. Frack's endowment is the largest, single private gift in BGSU's history. It is also the largest one-time gift ever designated to a Mid-American Conference basketball program. Thanks to Bill Frack for making a difference!

Making a Difference

The National Center for Missing and Exploited Children, (NCMEC) was created in 1984. It serves as the nation's resource on the issues of missing and sexually exploited children. The organization provides information and resources to law enforcement, parents, and children including child victims as well as other professionals. NCMEC began in a time of tragedy. According to their website, in 1979, six year old Ethan Patz disappeared from a New York street corner on his way to school and was never seen again. More children were abducted and murdered throughout the country. Then in 1981, six year old Adam Walsh was abducted from a Florida shopping mall and found brutally murdered. It should be noted that at this point in time police could enter information about stolen cars, stolen guns, and even stolen horses into the FBI's national crime computer – but not stolen children. That is no longer the case. More missing children come home safely today and more is being done today to protect children than any time in the nation's history. Check out the work of this amazing organization (missing-kids.com). NCMEC definitely makes a huge difference; find a way to make a difference to the kids in your life!

_____

_____

_____

_____

_____

Making a Difference

American writer Ruth Stafford Peale once said, "I consider it a priority anything that helps another person." Imagine if all of us started our day thinking this way. What a difference it would make!

_____

_____

_____

_____

_____

_____

_____

_____

_____

_____

_____

_____

_____

_____

_____

_____

_____

_____

_____

_____

Making a Difference

I have heard many people comment about how cooking for smaller groups of people is hard. These cooks still seem to make a lot of food and often wonder what to do with it. Here's an idea. How about purposefully preparing extra meals to freeze and have ready to offer someone who might be in need. Think about a friend who might have an illness in the family, a neighbor who is moving in or out, an elderly person who needs some attention, etc. By having these meals prepared and ready to go, you will be making a difference!

_____

_____

_____

_____

_____

_____

_____

_____

_____

_____

_____

_____

_____

_____

_____

Making a Difference

This month consider going to a senior center or assisted living center to visit, play games or simply hang out with the residents. Often times, many of these folks don't receive visitors and crave company as well as conversation. Organize your friends or family members to join you and make it a regular activity either every month or even year. By doing this you will be making a difference!

Making a Difference

Former Colorado Congresswoman Pat Schroeder said, "You can't wring your hands and roll up your sleeves at the same time." I love this statement. Stop wringing your hands and begin rolling up your sleeves. Find a way to help someone today! You will be making a difference!

Making a Difference

Cleric John Wesley, who is credited with his brother in having founded the Methodist movement, had the following service rule, "Do all the good you can; By all the means you can; In all the ways you can; In all the places you can; At all the times you can; To all the people you can; As long as you ever can." Imagine if we tried to do this every day. We would definitely know we were making a difference.

_____

_____

_____

_____

_____

_____

_____

_____

_____

_____

_____

_____

_____

_____

_____

_____

_____

Making a Difference

Garage, yard and tag sales given something away with no strings attached? My friend Renee does this all the time. If you admire something she is wearing, for example a necklace or pair of earrings, she will offer them to you with a very generous heart! Her generosity always makes a difference to both the giver and receiver. Thanks to Renee for leading by example.

Making a Difference

TIP OF THE DAY

𝒜n encouraging word or even an encouraging smile can make a person's day. Why not try to say at least one encouraging thing every day to someone. It will cost you nothing but definitely make a difference!

_____

_____

_____

_____

_____

_____

_____

_____

_____

_____

_____

_____

_____

_____

_____

_____

_____

_____

_____

_____

_____

_____

_____

Making a Difference

Have you heard of Warm Up America, a non-profit organization that has transformed thousands of lives? It began in a small town in Wisconsin with neighbors coming together to knit or crochet afghans for their neighbors in need in 1991. Since then, it has spread across the country. Its founder, Evie Rosen, decided that she would have volunteers knit or crochet small sections and then join them together. Today, afghans, caps and other items are distributed far and wide to folks in need. Check it out (warmupamerica.org). See how an idea in a small rural town has made a difference to thousands due to the generosity of knitters and crocheters across the country!

Making a Difference

I love to cook! While going out to eat is fun, I truly enjoy having people to my house to have a meal. I usually try a new recipe, hoping it turns out but realizing if it doesn't, it will still be all right. You see it is not about the food, but about spending time with people. That is what really makes the difference!

Making a Difference

Do you have a favorite charity? Why is it your favorite? At your next outing with friends make it a point to have a discussion about charities and causes near and dear to your heart. By simply starting the conversation, you will be making a difference!

Making a Difference

Do you plant a garden? If yes, this year consider planting a row for your favorite food bank, food pantry or soup kitchen. Simply add a row and when harvest time comes, donate the produce from this row to an organization that serves hungry people. How easy this idea is and what a wonderful way to make a difference!

Making a Difference

I love parades! I love the sights and sounds that accompany them. I also realize that most parades are a huge volunteer undertaking. This year consider becoming a volunteer for the local parade in your community. By volunteering, not only will you be up close and personal with the parade, but you will be making a difference!

Making a Difference

In the book about Olympic rowing, *The Amateurs*, the author David Halberstam writes, "When most oarsmen talked about their perfect moment in a boat, they referred not so much to winning a race but to the feel of the boat, all eight oars in the water together. The boat seemed to lift right out of the water. Oarsmen called that the moment of "swing." Imagine if we could get a "swing" with other volunteers, neighbors and friends in our philanthropic endeavors. What a difference "swing" could make in the world!

_____

_____

_____

_____

_____

_____

_____

_____

_____

_____

_____

_____

_____

_____

_____

Making a Difference

Growing Home is a Chicago-based nonprofit organization which assists the homeless, offers job training and creates employment opportunities for both the homeless and low income people. One training program is farming. The trainees learn all aspects of organic farming from growing vegetables to raising livestock. They also learn how to market their product at local farmers markets. Check it out (growinghomeinc.org) and see how Growing Home is making a difference!

Making a Difference

The great American storyteller Mark Twain said, "Kindness is the language which the deaf can hear and the blind can see." Make it your mission today to be kind to others and see what a difference you will be making not only in their world, but yours, too!

_____

_____

_____

_____

_____

_____

_____

_____

_____

_____

_____

_____

_____

_____

_____

_____

_____

_____

_____

Making a Difference

According to her brother, Princess Diana said, "A hug has no damaging side effects." Imagine if we lived in a world where kindness and things such as hugs were daily occurrences. What can you do today to bring more kindness into the world? Is it an encouraging word? Is it holding the door open for the person behind you? Is it simply smiling at everyone you meet? By doing any one of these acts or thousands of others, you will be making a difference!

Making a Difference

The "encore careers" movement is an effort to match older workers (who can't or don't want to retire) with jobs at nonprofit organizations. The movement began in the late 1990s and there are nonprofit organizations/programs that solely focus on this. Many of the programs are operated by people who have made the transition themselves. With more than 77 million Baby Boomers ages 46-65 this opportunity could explode and really transform the nonprofit sector. If you are a Baby Boomer, consider an encore career; you know you will be making a difference!

Making a Difference

The Food Depot, the food bank working to end hunger in Northern New Mexico (thefooddepot.org), holds an annual SouperBowl fundraising event! More than 25 chefs compete serving their best soups to more than 1200 people who vote which soup is the best! That chef/restaurant will then win the coveted SouperBowl trophy! What a fun way to support an outstanding nonprofit organization! By simply tasting soup, people are making a difference!

Making a Difference

Did you know when bad weather, such as snowstorms, floods, hurricanes, etc. hit an area the blood supply decreases dramatically? The American Red Cross (redcross. org) says when the snowstorms hit the East Coast hard in early 2011, the blood supply dropped to its lowest level in ten years! Impassable streets cause individuals to cancel their appointments to donate blood. Consider making a commitment to donate blood regularly, especially during inclement weather. You know you will be making a difference!

Making a Difference

In 2011, Microsoft founder Bill Gates declared that he was going to work to eliminate polio from our world. More than fifty years after the March of Dimes thought it had set a course to accomplish this, cases and even epidemics of the disease are being found in many countries throughout the world. Gates stated that this is his top priority and will work to secure world leaders to join him. Watch for the progress and see how one person's idea can lead to others working to make a difference!

Making a Difference

Have you heard of Polly Legendre and the CleanFish Company? CleanFish is a company with the mission of providing great seafood that is harvested from eco-friendly sources and water. Polly is a renowned chef who had her own catering business which she closed to join the mission focused CleanFish Company. Polly and CleanFish truly believe that every day they are making a difference in educating people about what we have done to our environment in harvesting fish and seafood. They work daily to improve fishing methods that are responsible and will lead to cleaner oceans and a healthier planet Earth. Polly and CleanFish are truly making a difference!

Making a Difference

In 2009 through the film *The Blind Side*, many of us learned the story about Michael Ohr and Leigh Ann Tuohy. Through this woman and her family as well as a young man's attitude, a life was transformed. What seemingly simple act, such as offering someone a place to sleep for the night, could you do today that would change someone's life forever? What could you do to make a difference?

Making a Difference

If you are of a certain age, you definitely remember the first time you saw the movie *Brian's Song*, which depicts the story of the lives of Chicago Bears players Brian Piccolo and Gale Sayers. In so many ways they made a difference. They were the first interracial players in the NFL to share a room. That alone was big news as it was the late 1960s and racial riots were raging throughout the country. What really happened was a friendship was formed that transcended all barriers. Find a copy of the original movie and watch it...perhaps again if you are of a certain age. Pay attention to how two seemingly very different men made a difference in each other's lives and ultimately to the rest of us!

_____

_____

_____

_____

_____

_____

_____

_____

_____

_____

_____

_____

My friend Chuck says that when he retires he wants to be a flower delivery man. He says, and I believe, that no matter what the occasion everyone loves getting flowers. Think about it. Simply giving flowers is a wonderful way to brighten someone's day and guaranteed to always make a difference!

Making a Difference

TIP OF THE DAY

Conserving the land is important. Land conservancies and land trusts are ways to help individuals insure the land they love is preserved in perpetuity primarily through conservation easements. If you have a large parcel of land that you would like preserved or know someone who does, consider working with your local land conservancy or trust. You can find the one in your area through a simple search on the Internet or by contacting your local community foundation. By conserving land for future generations, you will be making a difference!

Making a Difference

Think about this...instead of receiving presents for your birthday ask everyone to make a donation to either your favorite charitable cause or theirs. What a wonderful way to celebrate your birthday and make a difference to others!

Making a Difference

Each day brings the promise of possibilities. What will you do today to make a difference? How about telling someone that they made a difference in your life? Sometimes by simply telling someone they did something that matters makes all the difference!

_____

_____

_____

_____

_____

_____

_____

_____

_____

_____

_____

_____

_____

_____

_____

_____

_____

_____

_____

_____

_____

Making a Difference

Do you watch public television? There are wonderful programs about people making a difference. However, in order for it to remain available, charitable donations are needed. Consider adding your local public television station to your list of favorite causes. By making a donation, you will be making a difference!

_____

_____

_____

_____

_____

_____

_____

_____

_____

_____

_____

_____

_____

_____

_____

_____

_____

_____

_____

Making a Difference

My friend Peter is one of the most positive people I know. One of the ways he stays this way is by listening to music...all kinds of music. He believes it changes his mood and can change other people's moods, too. He says listening to music puts him in a good place and ready to tackle the world. Could listening to music put you in a good mood and ultimately lead you to make a difference today? Try it and see the effects!

Making a Difference

Every year, March 8th is International Women's Day celebrated annually since 1911. In 2011, the theme was "Equal access to education, training, science and technology. Pathway to decent work for women". What a wonderful way to recognize women and to support them in making a difference!

Making a Difference

When was the last time you went on a picnic with family and/or friends? Picnics and gatherings of people are a great way to stay connected. The simple act of getting together makes a difference on so many levels.

_____

_____

_____

_____

_____

_____

_____

_____

_____

_____

_____

_____

_____

_____

_____

_____

_____

_____

_____

_____

_____

_____

Making a Difference

Have you heard of the Go Red For Women Campaign? It is an effort by the American Heart Association to fight heart disease in women. As their website states, "Go Red For Women celebrates the energy, passion and power we have as women to band together to wipe out heart disease and stroke." One of the simple ways to participate is their Tell 5 Friends initiative. Go to the website (goredforwomen.org) and see how easy it is to inform your friends and family how to get healthy. You will be making a difference!

Making a Difference

I read an article in an airline magazine about an amazing act of kindness. It seems the Gainesville State School football team had an unusual group of fans one night. First you need to know that the Gainesville State School is a juvenile correctional facility with many of the students and hence players coming from broken homes. However, a number of the players had committed to football and the team as a way to refocus themselves and perhaps even restore their sense of self worth. Their season was winless; they did not have many fans nor did they hear many cheers. However, during one game against Faith Christian School of Grapevine, Texas, the Faith Christian School fans sat on the Gainesville side of the stadium cheering loudly for their school's opposing team. You might ask, "Why?" The simple answer was kindness. One only has to think for a moment of the amazing difference made that day to players who rarely had anyone cheering for them. The fans of Faith Christian School definitely made a difference to the Gainesville State School players and team!

Making a Difference

The Oscar-nominated actress Julianne Moore recalls that when she grew up at Halloween she would carry the UNICEF little orange box collecting money for the organization. That seemingly simple childhood act affected her long term, and after a trip in 2003 to Appalachia to help fight illiteracy and poverty among children, she started the Save the Children Valentine's Day Card Contest. Annually throughout the country, children draw Valentine's Day cards that are then voted on for the best. The five winners can be purchased (k2kusa.org) with the proceeds going to Save the Children! What a wonderful idea Julianne Moore had and an easy way to make a difference!

Making a Difference

Have you ever been reading something and realize you know the person. That is what happened to me when I was reading an article about a $40 glass of lemonade! Yes, it seems an acquaintance of mine named Ben was telling the story of how he paid $40 for a simple glass of lemonade. That drink was purchased at the 10th hole of the Make-A-Wish Foundation Golf Tournament in 1995. As the story goes, a little boy named Danny sold Ben the lemonade so that a "wish" could be granted. And it wasn't Danny's wish as his had already been fulfilled. He was doing this so another kid could have his wish experience! A young boy and a man, both working together to make a wish and a difference in this world!

Making a Difference

A 2008 report shows that most Americans believe nonprofit organizations are not financially efficient. Further, sixty-two percent thought charities spent too much on overhead expenses such as fundraising and administration costs. This is good information, and I encourage people to keep asking questions. But it is also important to keep donating while asking questions in order to insure nonprofit organizations are able to provide their services. By asking questions and donating, you will be making a difference!

Making a Difference

𝒜 recent survey resulted in 87% of Americans saying they believe corporations need to be more charitable and do more to promote social causes! According to the survey by the PR firm of Edelman, sixty-two percent of consumers say corporations need to do more than simply give away money. They need to integrate charitable causes and efforts into their day to day operations. I love it! Customers asking corporations to really make a difference!

Making a Difference

Have you heard of the Warrior's Wish Foundation located in New York? It was the result of a single person...a veteran who had cancer needed a bathroom built on the first floor of his house because he couldn't climb the stairs to the second floor. The local American Legion Post committed to constructing it and since then the group has made 100 wishes for veterans come true. What a way to make a difference!

_____

_____

_____

_____

_____

_____

_____

_____

_____

_____

_____

_____

_____

_____

_____

_____

_____

Making a Difference

TIP OF THE DAY

Children with autism are truly special people. However they and children with other developmental disabilities sometimes find a visit to the dentist office a scary prospect. Joshua Renken, a dentist located in Illinois, decided to do something about it. He started a nonprofit clinic, the Noll Dental Clinic, with the single goal of aiding this special group and doing so with kindness. He even takes it a step further and those who don't have insurance or can't pay the full amount, are asked to pay what they can. Thanks to Dr. Renken for making a difference!

Making a Difference

$\mathcal{S}uze\ \mathcal{O}rman,$ the well-known financial advisor, says, "I try to give things that get consumed because I don't want to add to anyone's clutter – a true gift doesn't burden the recipient." I love this statement and would add that making a donation in someone's name to their favorite charitable cause is a great way to achieve this goal and make a difference!

Making a Difference

The actress Demi Moore and actor Ashton Kutcher founded founded the DNA Foundation (demi-andashton.org), a nonprofit organization dedicated to stop the brokering of young girls for sex in the human trafficking trade. Slavery, in the form of human trafficking for sex, still exists throughout the world including the USA with the average age being 13. Thanks to Demi and Ashton for being leaders in bringing this difficult issue to the forefront of our attention. They are truly making a difference!

Making a Difference

As shared, human trafficking still continues today. Here are some facts: it is estimated that there are 27 million slaves throughout the world with half of them being under the age of 18. In the United States there is only one shelter dedicated to specifically meet the needs of trafficking victims. Spend time today learning more about this issue then find a way to make a difference!

Making a Difference

Grand Valley State University

Professor Salvatore (Sal) Alaimo is working on a documentary titled, "What is philanthropy?" Check out the trailer (whatisphilanthropy.org) then answer the question of how you will make a difference?

_____

_____

_____

_____

_____

_____

_____

_____

_____

_____

_____

_____

_____

_____

_____

_____

_____

_____

_____

_____

Making a Difference

I came across this and just like the saying. While the author is unknown, the statement is profound and true. It states, "Nobody can do everything, but everyone can do something." Just think if all of us did something to make a difference every day. What a difference it would make!

Making a Difference

Nelson Henderson is a person many of us have never heard of. According to his son, Wesley, Nelson was a quiet man with few words to say. However, on his graduation day, his son heard a profound statement from his father. He later wrote it to be shared with all of us. Nelson Henderson told his son, "The true meaning of life, Wesley, is to plant trees, under whose shade you do not expect to sit." That is truly making a difference!

_____

_____

_____

_____

_____

_____

_____

_____

_____

_____

_____

_____

_____

_____

_____

Making a Difference

The great poet, artist and author Khalil Gibran said, "You give but little when you give of your possessions. It is when you give of yourself that you truly give." Think about that statement and what you could give of yourself today that would make a difference. Perhaps it is a smile to a stranger, a ride to a neighbor or simply holding a door open for someone coming in behind you. All of these things do make a difference!

Making a Difference

Author Dan Bennett said, "Real charity doesn't care if it's tax deductible or not." How true! When we think about what we can do to make a difference does it really matter if it is a tax deduction? What can you do today to make a difference?

_____

_____

_____

_____

_____

_____

_____

_____

_____

_____

_____

_____

_____

_____

_____

_____

_____

_____

_____

_____

Making a Difference

Have you heard of service or volunteer vacations? It is an opportunity to do some work together, such as making a trail in a national forest, cleaning up a river, restoring a historic building, while vacationing. Many non-profit organizations are offering them and they are usually tax deductible. Think about it – truly a great way to take a vacation with friends or family and make a difference!

Making a Difference

Have you heard of the Silent Killer? Diabetes has often been called this. American musician, actor and director Bret Michaels tells of his fight with this disease by sharing he has had diabetes since the age of six and it has been a constant battle. Every year, diabetes kills more Americans than breast cancer and AIDS combined. Join the battle; learn your number and risk factor. By simply doing this you will be making difference!

_____

_____

_____

_____

_____

_____

_____

_____

_____

_____

_____

_____

_____

_____

_____

_____

_____

_____

Making a Difference

Women for Women International

is a nonprofit organization that has delivered over $50 million in microcredit loans and direct aid to women entrepreneurs in third world and developing country (womenforwomen.org). It is also a Conrad N. Hilton Humanitarian Prize recipient. This award is presented yearly to an organization that "significantly alleviates human suffering." Women for Women International is the first women's organization to receive this honor. Thanks to this group for making a difference!

Making a Difference

Do you want to recycle but your community doesn't have a program or provide containers and you don't know where to begin? There are nonprofit organizations that can provide assistance. First check this website (Earth911.org) to locate local recyclers. Dedicate a bin or two in your garage for recycling things like newspapers, plastic bottles and metal cans. By paying attention and taking these easy steps, you will be making a difference!

Making a Difference

Do you know where your food comes from? Most young people when asked this question will respond by saying the grocery story. Take time today to learn where and how food is grown and share this information, especially with younger people. They say the best food to eat is that which is locally grown. Visit the various farmers' markets in your community. You will be making a difference in so many ways.

_____

_____

_____

_____

_____

_____

_____

_____

_____

_____

_____

_____

_____

_____

_____

_____

Making a Difference

For more than 65 years, Heifer International has been working to help lift people out of poverty around the world. They do this by providing livestock to a family or individual, and you can help. Visit the Heifer International website (heifer.org) and select your gift...perhaps you would like to buy a cow, a flock of geese, a water buffalo, rabbits... the list goes on and on. You make your donation, select your gift and then watch how it works. Your gift will insure a family has food to eat and often food to trade (i.e., milk, eggs, butter, etc.). By doing this, you will definitely be making a difference!

Making a Difference

Have you considered becoming a Peace Corps volunteer? This program started in the 1960s under President John F. Kennedy with the sole purpose of making a difference in the world. In 2011, the 50th year of the Peace Corps was celebrated. Thanks to those visionaries and volunteers for making a difference!

Making a Difference

Are you and your family ready for a disaster? Are you prepared? Experts share that each of us should have 72 hours (three days) worth of food and water available at all times in our homes in case of a disaster. Check out the other suggestions to be ready for disaster (ready.gov). The tagline of this website is "Prepare. Plan. Stay Informed." By doing this you will be making a difference!

Making a Difference

Have you heard about Pay It Forward Day? Many have seen the movie or read the book *Pay It Forward*. It is a story about the young boy who did three good deeds for others in need. In return, all he wanted was for them to pass on the good deed to three other people and keep the cycle going. One good deed might not seem like much, but if everyone did something good for someone else, then the cycle of generosity and kindness could spark us to become better people. Pay it Forward Day is a powerful reminder of the positive difference we can all make, regardless of our age, background or wealth. Check it out (payitfowardday.com) for ideas of what you can do to participate...things such as paying for someone else's coffee or toll or feeding the parking meters of strangers. There are a lot of things you can do to pay it forward and it would make a difference!

Making a Difference

For more than eighteen years, the actor and Academy Award winner, Denzel Washington has been involved with the Boys and Girls Clubs serving as its national spokesperson. He credits this organization with helping him stay out of trouble during his youth. He sees even a greater need for this organization today. Take time this week to check out the Boys and Girls Clubs in your community. Consider involving your children or becoming involved yourself. As Denzel says, "Our children today are going where we lead them. We have a national crisis on our hands, but if every one of us gets involved, we can make a difference!"

TIP OF THE DAY

Struggling for what to give for gifts to certain people? Why not give a donation to their favorite charities. Check it out (justgive.org) for all your online giving. You will be amazed at how easy it is to make a difference!

Making a Difference

The Night Ministry (thenightministry.org) is a nonprofit organization that connects Chicago's vulnerable youth and adults by providing them with basic supplies, free healthcare, housing and support services. Its tagline is "Connecting at the Crossroads since 1976". I would add making a difference, too!

Making a Difference

Many of us became aware of the actor Leonardo DiCaprio through his film screen role as Jack Dawson in the blockbuster movie *Titantic*. What most people aren't aware of is that he is a passionate environmentalist and humanitarian! Along with others, he is looking for ways to raise consciousness about environmental issues. Leonardo even produced the documentary, *The 11th Hour*, about the crisis in the global ecosystem. Thanks to Leonardo for tackling such a huge issue and helping people to realize how they can make a difference!

Making a Difference

Many women struggle with finding information about their health issues. The nonprofit organization Healthy Women (heathywomen.org) provides free, unbiased information about health and well-being of women and their bodies. Check it out and see how information can help you make a difference!

Making a Difference

Francis Bacon was an English philosopher, statesman, scientist and lawyer who said, "In charity there is no excess." How true and if we practiced this message we would realize that no matter how large or small our charitable act is, it does make a difference!

Making a Difference

April is when many nonprofit organizations working and focused on Parkinson's disease try to raise the awareness of this illness. Parkinson's is a progressive brain disorder affecting more than six million people in the world and there is no cure! Emmy and Golden Globe Winner Michael J. Fox has dedicated his energies to this effort since being diagnosed with the disease in 1991 at age of 30. Michael J. Fox found a new way to make a difference!

_____

_____

_____

_____

_____

_____

_____

_____

_____

_____

_____

_____

_____

_____

_____

_____

_____

_____

Making a Difference

Since 1995, Martina McBride, the country music artist and songwriter, has hosted the YWCA Celebrity Auction each June as part of the CMA (County Music Association) Music Festival/Fan Fair. In 2010 the Auction raised more than $102,000 for the charity! Thanks Martina for working so hard to make a difference!

Making a Difference

Have you heard the story or seen the video of Johnny, the grocery store bagger? It is the story of how Johnny wanted to make a difference with the customers he served. He decided to write encouraging notes each night to place in each person's bag as he packed their groceries. What makes the story even more unique is that Johnny has Down syndrome. Take a few minutes to watch the video which can be found by searching the Internet for the words, "Johnny the bagger". While it is the story of customer service it is also the story of someone working daily to make a difference!

Making a Difference

April is Child Abuse Prevention Month. It is a subject most are uncomfortable discussing, but child abuse is a reality for many. Annually three million cases are reported in the USA, but it's estimated the number is three times higher. We must do better! Learn about CASA (Court Appointed Special Advocates), a nonprofit organization doing amazing work (casaforchildren.org), and find a way to help change a child's life! You will be making a difference!

Making a Difference

Dick Cavett, the talk show host and comedian, has openly talked about his bouts with clinical depression, which first affected him during his freshman year at college. His candor and honesty with his struggles has helped others in dealing with their depression. Think about if all of us were willing to share our stories, both the good stuff and the challenges, with others. It would definitely make a difference!

Making a Difference

April is the month designated as Autism Awareness Month. During April, a month-long effort is made to raise awareness about this disease. Let's look at some of the facts: Autism is a term used to describe five neurological disorders. One in 110 is the number of children diagnosed with some form of Autism. With boys that number is even higher with 1 in 70, meaning boys are four times more likely to be diagnosed with autism than girls. It is usually diagnosed in children before the age of three. Some feel this disease is growing at an epidemic rate as every twenty minutes someone is diagnosed with Autism. There are many nonprofit organizations working to help those directly affected and their families, including Autism Speaks and Easter Seals. Learn more today about this disorder and how you can help. Knowledge is a key to improving this situation and will help you find a way to make a difference!

_____

_____

_____

_____

_____

_____

_____

_____

_____

_____

_____

Making a Difference

Have you watched the documentary, Decoding Autism? According to my friend, Ann Brinkman Carstensen, "It's a wonderful film produced by PBS New Jersey that provides a thorough overview of the disease, what is known today about its symptoms and causes, and the research that still needs to be done. It's the best hour of television you'll ever watch." Check it out; take time to learn more. You will be making a difference!

Making a Difference

In 2011, the Melvindale High School (MI) girls' basketball team was #1 in their league, but that's not the position for which Coach Katie McFadden fought. She and her players realized the boys' teams had three referees per game and the girls only two. Katie worked with the Principal and Athletic Director to make this wrong right. They did this at Melvindale High School, but also took it further. The Downriver League to which they belonged upon realizing this inequality had an emergency meeting and said they are working to make it right for next year...that both boys and girls teams have the same number of referees per game as mandated by Title IX. Coach McFadden shows us one person can make a difference!

Making a Difference

I learned from my mom that Herb Alpert, the internationally renowned music artist and trumpeter who co-founded A and M Records, gave $500,000 to the Harlem School for the Arts after reading in a newspaper the school was about to close. Mom said he made a difference to her as she used to love to dance to his music at our little gray house in Montrose in the 1970s. Now he is making a difference to the next generation!

Making a Difference

𝒟𝑜 𝑦𝑜𝑢 𝑘𝑛𝑜𝑤 where to check out your favorite national nonprofit organization before making a donation? The Better Business Bureau's Wise Giving Alliance provides a charity seal of approval to those national nonprofit organizations meeting their 20 Standards for Charity Accountability. Check out your favorite national nonprofit organization via the Better Business Bureau's Wise Giving Alliance (give.org). Having more information is a way to make a difference!

Making a Difference

If you are like a lot of people, you like reading magazines and dislike simply throwing them in the garbage. It seems wasteful. Consider donating them to waiting rooms of your local hospital, doctor or dentist offices. Remember to remove the label with your name to protect yourself from identity theft. By donating your "already read" magazines you will be making a difference to many people!

Making a Difference

Most of us know the work Arianna Huffington is doing through her Huffington Post. Did you know she regularly posts about giving back? She said, "My sense of hope comes from the community level...wherever you find yourself there is something you can give." What a great mantra to live by and guaranteed to make a difference!

_____

_____

_____

_____

_____

_____

_____

_____

_____

_____

_____

_____

_____

_____

_____

_____

_____

_____

_____

Making a Difference

Did you know teachers spend about $500 of their own money on school supplies for their classrooms annually? Do you want to help? There is an organization that can assist you. Check out the organization via its website (iloveschools.com) and type in your zip code to find a school near you in need of supplies. What a great way to make a difference!

Making a Difference

If you have children, you've probably experienced at some point an explosion of stuffed animals. What can you do with them once your child outgrows them? Consider donating them to SAFE (stuffedanimalsforemergencies.org) a nonprofit organization that gives them to homeless shelters, hospitals as well as EMT workers who use them when they meet kids on their calls. It is a great way to make a difference!

Making a Difference

People over 55 have a wealth of experience! Senior Corps is a nonprofit dedicated to connecting them with service organizations that can use their skills. Conceived during JFK's administration, more than 500,000 people serve as mentors, coaches and companions helping others in need. Check it out (seniorcorps.org); find out how seniors are making a difference!

Making a Difference

When traveling and staying at hotels do you take the little bottles of shampoo, lotion, etc. only to find them in a drawer months later unused? Consider donating them to your local domestic violence shelter. They are always in need of toiletry supplies. If you don't travel, consider purchasing shampoo, soap, lotion, etc. and making a donation that way. Either way will definitely be making a difference

Former Secretary of State Condoleezza

Rice said, "It is a dangerous thing to ask why someone else has been given more. It is humbling – and indeed healthy – to ask why you have been given so much." What a wonderful way to look at life. What could you do with all you have been given to make a difference?

_____

_____

_____

_____

_____

_____

_____

_____

_____

_____

_____

_____

_____

_____

_____

_____

_____

_____

Making a Difference

Animal shelters exist to take care of stray or unwanted animals, primarily cats and dogs. If you are considering getting a cat or dog, visit your local animal shelter first. You just might find the pet you are looking for while making a difference!

Making a Difference

The American writer and poet Carl Sandburg is credited with saying, "Nothing happens unless first a dream." How very true! What dreams do you have to change the world or to change something in your community? How can you make your dream come true? What can you do today to make a difference?

_____

_____

_____

_____

_____

_____

_____

_____

_____

_____

_____

_____

_____

_____

_____

_____

_____

_____

_____

_____

_____

_____

Making a Difference

The former First Lady of the United States, Lady Bird Johnson, said, "Become so wrapped up in something that you forget to be afraid." What if each of us found something with which to become that involved? What a difference it would make!

Making a Difference

Benjamin Franklin, one of the Founding Fathers, said, "One today is worth two tomorrows." Think about what you are putting off until tomorrow that could help your community or someone. Could you do it today and make a difference?

_____

_____

_____

_____

_____

_____

_____

_____

_____

_____

_____

_____

_____

_____

_____

_____

_____

_____

_____

_____

Making a Difference

Theodore Roosevelt, the 26th President of the United States, said, "Do what you can, with what you have, where you are." How profound and true! Too often I hear folks putting off things until something happens or changes. If you follow Teddy's advice, you will definitely be making a difference every day!

Making a Difference

What are you going to do with your wedding gown? Is your daughter or niece really going to wear it? Brides Against Breast Cancer is a nonprofit organization that collects bridal gowns and organizes sales through a national tour. This tour offers brides to be an opportunity to purchase a bridal gown at a greatly reduced cost. The upside is that the proceeds go to grant wishes to women and men who have terminal breast cancer. Check it out (bridesagainstbreastcancer.org) and see how donating your bridal gown can make a difference!

Making a Difference

Many of us grew up learning how to play a musical instrument. We may have even played that instrument well into our high school and college years. My guess is that a lot of us have our old musical instruments tucked away in the closet unused for years and now gathering dust. Consider donating it to your local school or music program as they are often in need of instruments for those students whose families cannot afford to purchase one. Music is a gift we should have access to and many don't because their family circumstances don't allow them the opportunity to purchase a musical instrument. By donating or recycling your old saxophone, trumpet, clarinet or flute, you will be passing on the gift of music and making a difference!

Making a Difference

Have you heard about The Children's Book Project? It is a nonprofit organization founded to provide books to children. To date, more than 1.5 million gently used books have been given to children who need them. Check it out (childrensbookproject.org). Then go through your books or bookshelves at home to see if you might be able to make a donation and thus make a difference!

_____

_____

_____

_____

_____

_____

_____

_____

_____

_____

_____

_____

_____

_____

_____

_____

_____

_____

_____

Making a Difference

Have you heard of Mission Fish? It is the way to fundraise for your favorite nonprofit organization on eBay. In 2010, more than $54 million was donated to charities through this program. Check it out (missionfish.org) and see if there is a way for you to participate and make a difference!

Making a Difference

Do you have soccer equipment that is leftover from your kids when they played lying around the house or garage? Consider donating it to Peace Passers (peacepassers.org) a nonprofit organization that collects gently used soccer equipment and donates it to communities in need throughout the world. You will be accomplishing two things – cleaning a part of your house or garage while making a difference!

Making a Difference

Riders For Health is a nonprofit organization headquartered in Great Britain that is doing amazing work in Africa. According to their website, "In Africa millions of people are dying from easily-preventable diseases because health workers do not have the reliable transport to reach them. By ensuring health workers have access to vehicles that never break down Riders For Health is making sure millions of people across Africa receive regular, reliable health care, often for the first time in their lives." Check out this nonprofit organization (riders.org) and learn how others are working to make a difference!

Making a Difference

Community colleges are an important and often overlooked resource available to us. Check out the community college in your geographic area. There are often relevant and timely programs with classes and opportunities open to all. I am the proud graduate of the community college system in Michigan (Alpena Community College) and can wholeheartedly say they do make a difference!

Making a Difference

Have you ever heard the saying one person's trash is another person's treasure? The nonprofit organization Freecycle has found a way to make this saying a reality and keep stuff out of the landfills locally. Freecycle has eight million members focused on what they call "worldwide gifting". The goal is to reduce trash bound household items such as bikes, coffee tables, appliance, birthday and holiday decorations, etc. by connecting these items to folks who want them. Check it out (freecycle.org) and see how you can participate. By doing so you will be making a difference on many different levels!

_____

_____

_____

_____

_____

_____

_____

_____

_____

_____

_____

_____

_____

_____

Making a Difference

Detroit and the surrounding metro area are focused on coming back from this recession. It is an area with many hidden gems including the Henry Ford Museum located in Dearborn, Michigan. Check it out (thehenryford.org) and consider planning a visit. By making a trip to Michigan, which is severely economically challenged these days, you will be making a difference on so many levels!

Making a Difference

Singer, actress, director and Grammy Award winner Barbra Streisand is considered a philanthropic all star! She donated $21 million from her last two concert tours to a variety of causes she supports. Recently she launched a $10 million fundraising campaign to support the Women's Heart Center at Cedars-Sinai Heart Institute located in Los Angeles saying she will match funds up to $5 million. Barbra says she was surprised to learn that heart disease kills more women than all cancers combined. Barbra Streisand is definitely working to make a difference!

Making a Difference

The MusiCares Foundation is part of the National Academy of Recording Arts and Sciences (NARAS) better known as the Grammys. Its mission is to help support members of the music industry in times of financial, medical and personal need. Annually it bestows a Person of the Year honor on a musician as part of the Grammy Awards festivities and fundraising efforts. Look for it next year and see how musicians are making sure they are taking care of each other. MusiCares definitely makes a difference in the music world!

Making a Difference

Barbra Streisand is quoted as saying,
"People's generosity has been wonderful and inspiring."
Where and when are you inspired by people's generosity?
Who is making a difference in your community or world?

_____

_____

_____

_____

_____

_____

_____

_____

_____

_____

_____

_____

_____

_____

_____

_____

_____

_____

_____

_____

TIP OF THE DAY

Courage is the virtue I value most! The beloved actor John Wayne is quoted as saying, "Courage is being scared to death – but saddling up anyway." Is there something happening or not happening in your community that you have been afraid to tackle? Is there something you can do to affect change that will help others? Saddle up and muster your courage to make a difference today!

Making a Difference

The French-Cuban author Anais Nin said, "Life shrinks or expands in proportion to one's courage." Think about what you could do today to change someone's life. Then have the courage to make a difference. Your life will definitely be expanded by your willingness to make a difference!

Making a Difference

My cousin, Kim, gave me a gift of a paper-weight with the following statement on it, "The secret of happiness is freedom and the secret of freedom is courage." What does your freedom afford you to do today that would take courage, lead to happiness and definitely make a difference?

_____

_____

_____

_____

_____

_____

_____

_____

_____

_____

_____

_____

_____

_____

_____

_____

_____

_____

Making a Difference

The famed and beloved actor John Wayne said, "Give the American people a good cause, and there's nothing they can't lick." He beat lung cancer in 1965 and then fifteen years later he fought a battle against stomach cancer which eventually took his life. After his death from cancer, his family in 1985 created The John Wayne Cancer Foundation. Its mission is to bring courage, strength and grit to the fight against cancer. It does this through funding research, treatment and education. Check it out (teamduke.org) and see how the Duke through this foundation continues to make a difference!

Making a Difference

John Wayne, the famous actor and director, said, "Tomorrow is the most important thing in life. Comes into us at midnight very clean. It's perfect when it arrives and it puts itself in our hands. It hopes we've learned something from yesterday." Think about the opportunity each day presents us to make a difference!

Making a Difference

Recently a man shared with me the story of his daughter giving up three months of her life to go to Peru to help pregnant women. She was helping women learn about better health practices. He was amazed and awed by her willingness to give back at such a young age! What a shining example! But you don't have to go to Peru — what can you do in your neighborhood to make a difference?

Making a Difference

Today there are more than 650,000 homeless people. In New York City alone, it is estimated that more than 80% of them are women. We must do better! Learn more today about the homeless problem in your community then find a way to make a difference!

Making a Difference

Microsoft founder Bill Gates has a list of eleven rules he shares with young people. Rule Number Five states "Flipping burgers is not beneath your dignity. Your grandparents had a different word for burger flipping: they called it opportunity." What opportunities are presented to you in the form of something you might initially decline or think beneath your dignity? Consider taking on the "opportunity" as it might make a difference!

Making a Difference

Did you know that ten million people worldwide are living with HIV and in need of treatment? Grammy Award winning singer/songwriter Alicia Keys co-founded the nonprofit organization Keep a Child Alive (keepachildalive. org). Its mission is to provide medicine for HIV and support for AIDS orphans in Africa and India. She is also involved with Frum Tha Ground Up (ftgu.org) which encourages youth in the United States to complete their education. Alicia Keys is finding many ways to make a difference!

Making a Difference

Do you ever visit old cemeteries? Old cemeteries are filled with people who lived amazing lives. Take time to learn about the people in your community's cemetery. If there are tours with a docent, take one to learn about the unique ways those who are buried, when they lived, made a difference!

Making a Difference

Many of us recall hearing about the thirteen year old girl who was surfing when she was attacked by a shark and lost her arm. Her dream was to be a professional surfer and a month after the attack she was back in the ocean learning how to rebalance herself and surf with one arm! In 2007 she became a professional surfer and now travels the world after having won a national surfing championship. In the nine years since her attack, she has written and published five books about her sense of spirituality. Check them out. Her name is Bethany Hamilton and she has definitely made a difference!

Making a Difference

Since 2001, actress and humanitarian Angelina Jolie has been the United Nation's Advocate for refugees. As of 2011, she has visited more than twenty countries. She is a highly visible celebrity and uses that status to bring awareness to an issue that might otherwise go unnoticed. Thanks Angelina for making a difference!

Making a Difference

Are you a lifelong learner? If not, consider becoming one. As we grow older, we usually read in our area of comfort be it magazines, newspapers, fiction or nonfiction books. Consider purposefully reading outside your comfort zone. In other words, pick up books and materials that you normally would not read or peruse. By this simple act, you will be making a difference!

Making a Difference

Andrew Carnegie was known as a smart businessman and an outstanding philanthropist. During his lifetime, he was known as the second richest man after John D. Rockefeller. With his success in steel business having founded Carnegie Steel Company, he donated most of his money to establishing more than 3000 public libraries in English speaking countries such as the United States, Canada, Great Britain as well as other countries. Andrew Carnegie's impact lasts until today. He definitely made a difference!

Making a Difference

Matt Damon is a famous actor and Academy Award Winner as well as a philanthropist. Following his 2006 film *Running the Sahara*, which depicted the water crisis in North Africa, he founded H20 Africa (in July 2009 it merged with another group and became known as water.org) which provides micro loans to communities for wells and sanitation. He is also involved with Feeding America as a spokesperson, serving on its Entertainment Council. Matt Damon is definitely making a difference!

Making a Difference

Could the business or company you work for sponsor one day of disaster relief in your community? It's easy to do. Basically, you conduct an effort for one month to pay for a day of disaster relief in your county. It's really simple ..take the amount of disaster relief dollars spent in the previous year in your county and divide it by 365 days. You can challenge all businesses and even organizations in your county to sponsor as many days as they can. Contact your local American Red Cross (redcross.org) to see how you might begin this effort and work to make a difference!

Making a Difference

My dad's favorite saying was one from the 1970s. Do you remember the phrase, "Keep on truckin'"? I think sometimes this is the attitude we need to have when working in the nonprofit world. We need to keep on truckin' to make a difference!

Making a Difference

Most people know Will Allen for his skill as a national professional basketball player. What most people don't know is his roots are in farming as his family grew a lot of the food they ate while he was growing up. As an adult this has become a passion of his, and he founded the nonprofit organization Growing Power (growingpower.org) which works to transform communities by supporting people in the development of community food systems. Will Allen says, "If people can grow safe, healthy, affordable food, if they have access to land and clean water, this is transformative on every level in a community. I believe we cannot have healthy communities without a healthy food system." Thank you Will Allen for working to make a difference every day!

Making a Difference

Have you seen those billboards from the Foundation for a Better Life? They say things such as "Still Serving" - Giving Back and show a picture of Andre' Agassi or have the words, "The longest journey begins with one small step" - Achievement and depicts a picture of Neil Armstrong and his first step on the moon. Pay attention to these billboards and do as it suggests, "Pass it on". You will be making a difference!

Making a Difference

The Foundation for a Better Life

website collects stories from people about things that made a difference in their lives. I was reading some of them and found this one from a girl named Bianca. She wrote, "There was a girl in my gym class. Everyone considered her a total spaz when it came to kick ball or basketball. So when we had to choose teams, I was team captain. I had the first choice and my friends told me before hand not to choose the girl. Well I saw the girl standing there away from the whole class so I chose her first. Everyone else got angry at me, but I didn't care. That day my team, which was full of all the "losers", "weirdoes" and "outcasts" won the basketball game. Even though it was just gym we all felt as if we just won the Olympics." Thanks to Bianca for sharing her story and for finding an amazing way to make a difference

---

Making a Difference

Sometimes the simplest acts of kindness can make a difference. In reading stories posted by individuals on the Foundation for a Better Life website, I came across one that illustrated this point. While the author is anonymous, it still makes the point. The storyteller said, "I was returning from another business trip, heading to my car. A five-year-old boy stood at the top of the escalator. At first, I thought he was just playing, but as I got closer, I realized his mom was half-way down the escalator. She thought he was right behind her and his little sister. When she turned around and saw her son there, she started pleading with him to get on the escalator. He just shook his head no. So I said "Want some help?" He nodded his head yes, and took my hand. We held hands all the way down the escalator. He told me that he liked the moving sidewalks, but didn't like escalators...they are pretty scary. There was a relieved Mom at the bottom. My kids are grown now, but I still remember those frantic days with multiple small kids, and was glad for the opportunity to provide a little relief." A simple way that someone made a difference!

_____

_____

_____

_____

_____

_____

Making a Difference

What do Sidney Kimmel, Mark Zuckerberg and Denny Sanford have in common? They are among the wealthiest individuals signing the Giving Pledge. The Giving Pledge asks its signatories to publicly commit to giving away the majority of their wealth during their lifetime! What stirs my heart is many of these people are entrepreneurs who made a difference in business and are now making a difference in philanthropy!

Making a Difference

Hunger is a constant for more than 50 million Americans. You probably know someone who is food insecure and doesn't know where they will find their next meal. Feeding America, the largest domestic hunger-relief organization, is made up of more than 200 food banks that feed the hungry in virtually every community in the country 365 days a year. Check out (feedingamerica.org) and learn how far your financial donation can go. Every dollar donated to Feeding America helps provide eight meals to people in need. Make a financial donation to help the hungry. You will be making a difference!

_____

_____

_____

_____

_____

_____

_____

_____

_____

_____

_____

_____

_____

_____

Making a Difference

The United States has one of the most extensive national park systems in the world. Did you know there are more than 84.4 million acres in the national parks? The national parks are often referred to as national treasures and the more well known parks referenced as the "crown jewels" of the park system. What most people don't know is that you can make a charitable donation to the National Park System (nps.gov). Check it out and consider making a donation. I guarantee by doing so you will be making a difference for generations to come!

Making a Difference

Grammy Award Winning Musician Eric Clapton recently sold dozens of his guitars and amps at a New York auction to benefit an alcohol and drug treatment center he founded in Antigua. Clapton is a recovering addict who previously had established the Crossroads Centre in the West Indies in 1998. Eric Clapton made a difference in music and now is selling his guitars to make a difference to others!

Making a Difference

Garth Brooks had a great impact on country music. I love the song he wrote titled, "We Shall Be Free". He wrote it after being in Los Angeles (LA) for the Academy of Country Music (ACM) Awards in 1992 and watching the LA Riots. He wrote, "The night the riots hit we watched it all on TV on the bus leaving LA. And as you drove out of LA you could see the buildings on fire. It was pretty scary for all of us, especially a bunch of guys from Oklahoma. Ya know this is intense out here." Here is the beginning of the song. "This ain't comin' From no prophet Just an ordinary man When I close my eyes I see the way This world shall be When we all walk Hand in hand When the last child Cries for a crust of bread When the last man dies For just words that he said When there's shelter Over the poorest head We shall be free We shall be free We shall be free Stand straight, Walk proud, Have a little faith, Hold out We shall be free We shall be free We shall be free Stand straight, Have a little faith We shall be free." By observing the riots and responding to them by writing these lyrics, Garth Brooks definitely made a difference!

Making a Difference

One day I was at the small airport in my hometown of Alpena, Michigan. I was patiently waiting for my plane to arrive so I could board it and depart. It arrived and I watched the people departing the plane and others greeting them, I saw a man standing far back from the door through which passengers were entering the airport from the plane. It was obvious he was waiting for someone with a bit of cautiousness. Curious, I paid attention to him and saw his body posture change immediately when a young, military dressed man got off the plane and walked toward the door to the airport. What was amazing to witness was when the young man came through the door, he literally ran to his dad and a full, hearty embrace took place. The scene that day by that father and son made a difference to me. Two men embracing after having been separated for a period of time due to one of them serving their country. It reminded me that every day is important and we need to remember to recognize those days and moments that make a difference!

Making a Difference

Have you ever read the obituaries? It is fascinating what we learn about people after they die. Troy Patterson commented in *Slate* stating, "...wouldn't it be great if they instead...published profiles of these remarkable people on their 80th birthdays? That way the fascinated reader would have a chance to call up a fascinating oldster and chat." What a wonderful idea, but we don't have to wait. Think about who has made a difference in your life then call them to talk. You will definitely be making a difference in their life!

_____

_____

_____

_____

_____

_____

_____

_____

_____

_____

_____

_____

_____

_____

_____

_____

_____

_____

Making a Difference

I love the movies and especially movies about the Holocaust and survival. In reading about how the movie *Defiance*, which is about the Bielski brothers, was developed I was amazed. If you saw the movie, you know it is about four brothers who saved Jews in what is now Belarus. It is estimated they helped and saved more than 1200 Jews. What was interesting was the obituary of the older brother, Tuvia. It simply said that after the war he had worked first as a truck driver then as a cab driver. It made me think of all the times I have been impatient when a truck driver was moving his truck too slow or blocking the street; or the times I ignored a cab driver not even asking how he (or she) was doing. What if one of those times it had been Tuvia or someone who had done something to make a difference in the lives of others? The story reminded me that is it important to recognize that every person can and does make a difference!

Making a Difference

$\mathcal{I}$ attended the Tribute to Achievement fundraising dinner for the Girls Scouts of Greater Chicago and Northwest Indiana (gsgcnwi.org). I learned it's estimated that 89% of all women were at one time Girl Scouts and even more amazing that all of the women astronauts were Girl Scouts, too! Almost 100 years ago a woman named Juliette Gordon Low had a vision and started the Girl Scouts! What a difference it has made!

Making a Difference

Do you love Girl Scout cookies? Did you know the Girl Scouts' Cookies Program is the largest financial literacy program in the world for girls? Did you realize that selling Girl Scout cookies not only helps the troops raise money but also teaches the young girls about business? Annually more than $700 million worth of cookies are sold and girls of all ages learn about selling, marketing, distribution, inventory control, accounts receivable, accounts payable, budgeting, collections, etc. Girls Scouts are still making a difference!

_____

_____

_____

_____

_____

_____

_____

_____

_____

_____

_____

_____

_____

_____

_____

Making a Difference

Have you heard of the John F. Kennedy Service Awards? The awards are given every five years to people who have worked for the Peace Corps and have demonstrated a commitment to community service abroad and in the United States. Do you know someone who fits this profile? If you do, nominate them for this award. While they have already made a difference through their life's work to help others, you can make a difference in their life by nominating them for this award.

Making a Difference

I saw a half page ad in the *Chicago Tribune* with a picture of Itzhak Perlman, the great virtuoso violinist. He was looking directly at the reader with his thumb and index finger spread about 1 inch apart. The phrase by his hand said, "We are this close to ending polio." The ad highlighted the work of Rotary International and reminded us that polio still cripples thousands of children worldwide. Their goal is to "...wipe this disease off the face of the earth forever." Check out how the effort is going (rotary.org/endpolio). Perhaps there is a way to help and make a difference!

Making a Difference

Do you live in a place that doesn't allow animals? Does your work life make it highly impractical for you to have a dog or a cat as a pet? Animal shelters are a great place to fulfill your desire to have access to pets and volunteer! Animal shelters are always in need of people to help care for the stray and unwanted animals. Consider becoming a volunteer and you will be making a difference!

Making a Difference

I read in the book *Switch: How to Change Things When Change is Hard* that, "...big changes come from a succession of small changes." Sometimes problems in our community seem overwhelming and at times impossible to solve or resolve. What small change or step could you take today that would ignite the process of change with an issue that faces your world? What can you do to make a difference today?

_____

_____

_____

_____

_____

_____

_____

_____

_____

_____

_____

_____

_____

_____

_____

_____

_____

Making a Difference

Often times we won't start something because we think we might fail. But what if you succeeded? What if your efforts made the change that needs to happen? Failure is a part of success...you have to try to make a difference!

Making a Difference

I learned about a high school principal who took the job knowing that eighty-five percent (85%) of the students did not go to college and were not considered successful. The school had a new building, but needed a new attitude and focus. While lots of changes were made, the biggest was the discontinuation of failing grades. Students could only receive the following grades: A, B, C and NY. NY meant Not Yet. With the new system students knew teachers expected more of them and guess what happened...the students performed. In 2008, Molly Howard, principal of Jefferson County High School in Louisville, Georgia was named US Principal of the Year out of 48,000 candidates! Principal Howard made a difference!

_____

_____

_____

_____

_____

_____

_____

_____

_____

_____

_____

_____

Making a Difference

There is a famous story about IBM and its culture of trying new things and accepting failure as an option. In the 1960s, an employee at the executive level made a decision that caused the company to lose $10 million ($70 million in 2009 dollars). Tom Watson, who was the CEO at that time, met with the employee inquiring if he knew why he had been summoned to his office. The employee responded that he thought he was going to be fired. To which Tom Watson immediately replied, "Fire you? I just spent $10 million educating you." What big mistakes have you made that you can learn from to continue making a difference in your community?

Making a Difference

Have you heard of The Valerie Fund? It was started in 1976 by a nine year old girl named Valerie Goldstein. When she was ill, Valerie had to travel long distances to receive treatment. She and her parents were committed to changing this paradigm. The mission of The Valerie Fund is to provide support for comprehensive health care for children with cancer and blood disorder; not only to the child but to the entire family because when a child is ill, it does affect the entire family. Check it out (valeriefund.org). Thanks to Valerie and her parents for taking something that affected them and making a difference to so many.

Making a Difference

The Harlem Children's Zone (hcz.org)

is doing whatever it takes to educate children and strengthen the community! Started by Geoffrey Canada, his vision as shared on their website began in the early 1990s, "HCZ ran a pilot project that brought a range of support services to a single block. The idea was to address all the problems that poor families were facing: from crumbling apartments to failing schools, from violent crime to chronic health problems." One single man seeing an opportunity and making a difference to more than 10,000 children and 7400 adults annually!

_____

_____

_____

_____

_____

_____

_____

_____

_____

_____

_____

_____

_____

_____

Making a Difference

The Alzheimer's Association is working daily to combat this disease. As shared on their website, "Our vision is a world without Alzheimer's disease." Learn more about the disease and the warning signs by visiting the website (alz.org). Find out how you can help to make a difference!

Making a Difference

Helen Keller is always an inspiration and she definitely made a difference! One of my favorite quotes from her is, "No pessimist ever discovered the secrets of the stars, or sailed to an uncharted land, or opened a new heaven to the human spirit." This statement is a great mantra to remember as you go about your day. Use your optimism to make a difference!

Making a Difference

The great American poet and author Maya Angelou said, "If you don't like something, change it. If you can't change it, change your attitude." What a statement to live by; what a way to make a difference!

_____

_____

_____

_____

_____

_____

_____

_____

_____

_____

_____

_____

_____

_____

_____

_____

_____

_____

_____

_____

Making a Difference

Did you watch the television show in the spring of 2011 called *Secret Millionaire*? What was amazing to me was the number of individuals, from all walks of life, working to make a difference in the lives of other people and their communities. Everyday people seeing an opportunity to change their world and being willing to sacrifice to make a difference! What can you do today to make a difference to someone else today?

Brian Aldiss, the English author of fiction and science fiction works, said, "Whatever creativity is, it is part of the solution to a problem." What a profound and true statement! How can you use your creativity today to be part of a solution to a problem and eventually make a difference?

Making a Difference

Most of us have seen or are aware of the movies *Dr. Zhivago* and *A Man for All Seasons*. Did you know their adaption won Robert Bolt, the writer of both movies, two Academy Awards? He is quoted with saying, "Doin' nothing's a dangerous occupation." How many of us have asked ourselves where to start when faced with a problem? If we do nothing it can be dangerous! Do something today to make a difference!

Making a Difference

American civil rights leader and women's suffragist Susan B. Anthony said, "Organize, agitate, educate, must be our war cry." What can you do today to shake things up to make a difference in your world or community?

_____

_____

_____

_____

_____

_____

_____

_____

_____

_____

_____

_____

_____

_____

_____

_____

_____

_____

_____

_____

_____

TIP OF THE DAY

Johann Wolfgang Von Goethe was a German writer whose works spanned poetry, literature, philosophy and science. He is quoted as saying, "A man can stand almost anything except a success of ordinary days." I find this statement to be true. Work to make your days extraordinary! Do it by purposefully find a way to make a difference everyday!

Making a Difference

Have you ever heard of the nonprofit organization Common Sense (commonsense.com)? It works to help kids and their parents thrive in a world of media and technology. Think of all the ways children encounter the media every day. Media can inspire and bring joy, but there can also be serious side effects. Check out how this nonprofit organization is working to make a difference to kids and their parents.

_____

_____

_____

_____

_____

_____

_____

_____

_____

_____

_____

_____

_____

_____

_____

Making a Difference

Queen Latifah first broke into the public arena as a hip hop artist then quickly gained fame through her acting and writing. Did you know she is also a dedicated philanthropist? In 2011 during a speech she said, "Sometimes people have to step back and ask themselves whose feelings are really going to be hurt by not helping someone out. To me, helping others is worth it every time. If I can bring someone joy, I will assist them whenever they are in need. I'm very thankful to have this opportunity." Dana Owens (whose stage name is Queen Latifah) definitely makes a difference!

Making a Difference

Dana Owens, known to most of us at Queen Latifah, is an outstanding philanthropist. She has shared her story of her first philanthropic experience. When she was young as she and her friends would go to the Boys and Girls Club in her hometown of Newark, New Jersey. She credits the inviting environment and friendships formed there with having long lasting impact on her life. She says it fostered willingness if not a necessity to help others the way she had been helped in her youth. Thanks to the Boys and Girls Clubs throughout the country for teaching philanthropy and helping children to learn how to make a difference!

Making a Difference

When Queen Latifah was eight years old, she learned the power of philanthropy. During a speech she gave to the AFP (Association of Fundraising Professionals) International Conference, Queen Latifah shared that when she was a child she would share her lunch with classmates or collect pennies that could help others. Since an early age, Queen Latifah has been making a difference!

Making a Difference

Ever think of holding a "Preparedness Week"? You or your employer could have a different preparedness topic for each day of the week and provide that to employees and customers. Suggestions could be made every day encouraging each employee do one thing per day to make their home and family prepared for an emergency. What a simple way to make a difference!

Making a Difference

Have you ever considered having an effort with your co-workers to collect comfort kits for victims of disasters? In times of upheaval and trouble, something as simple as a toothbrush, toothpaste, soap and shampoo can have a tremendous impact on how a person deals with the situation they are facing. Check out what is in most comfort kits and how to begin by going to the American Red Cross website (redcross.org). You can make a difference!

_____

_____

_____

_____

_____

_____

_____

_____

_____

_____

_____

_____

_____

_____

_____

_____

_____

_____

Making a Difference

It is reported that approximately 70% of the firefighters in the United States are volunteers! Yes, men and women volunteering to help their neighbors in times of fire and distress. What a gift they provide to all of us! Thank you to the volunteers who sign up for this work. They truly are making our communities a safer place to live and definitely making a difference!

Making a Difference

Actor, director, producer, writer and Academy Award Winner George Clooney is often more noted for using his celebrity status towards his humanitarian, social activism and philanthropic endeavors. One only has to think of the 2010 devastating Haiti earthquake to recall that it was George who pulled everyone together for the Hope for Haiti concert/telethon. He also raised funds for the 2004 Tsunami as well as for the victims of the 9/11. He currently is focused on the crisis in Sudan. When he travels, the paparazzi follows and George realized he could parlay that into good by traveling to areas that needed issues highlighted. By using all he has at his disposal, George Clooney is making a difference

Making a Difference

Do you know what is in your cosmetics and personal care products? Recently, I learned that there are many toxins, including carcinogens, in cosmetics and personal care products and that industry is not regulated by an outside agency or group but rather regulates itself. There is lead in many lipsticks and toxic chemicals even in baby shampoo! Check out the nonprofit organization the Campaign for Safe Cosmetics (safecosmetics.org); watch the short video and you will be amazed at what you learn! You can begin to make a difference by becoming knowledgeable about the products you use every day!

_____

_____

_____

_____

_____

_____

_____

_____

_____

_____

_____

_____

_____

_____

Making a Difference

Have you heard of the nonprofit organization called Cease Fire? It is a national public health strategy proven to make communities safer by reducing the shootings and killings in neighborhoods. It is an interdisciplinary model contending that violence is a learned behavior and can be changed. It began in 2000 in the area of West Garfield Park in Chicago, one of the most violent areas of the city. In its first year, shootings were reduced by 67%! Check it out (ceasefirechicago.org) and learn how this nonprofit organization is making a difference!

Making a Difference

Everyday many people in our communities are hungry. The faces of hunger include children, families and the elderly, most likely people living in your neighborhood that you do not realize are skipping meals because they simply cannot afford food for every person in the family for each meal. Learn more about hunger in your community by going to the Feeding America website (feedingamerica.org) and locating the food bank that is doing work in your area to feed hungry people. Hunger happens every single day, not just during the holiday season. Discover how you can get involve to make a difference!

Making a Difference

Have you ever really thought about kids who receive free and reduced lunches in school? For too many children, those school lunches are the only meals they can count on getting regularly. Evenings, weekends and school holidays can be a struggle for families, because when school is out, those meals are unavailable. Many food banks support backpack programs, which send children home with discreet packs full of nonperishable, kid-friendly food to eat on weekends and holidays. Contact your local food bank to learn how you can help feed children in need usually for as little as $60 a year. Your help will make a difference in a child's life!

Making a Difference

I attended the annual meeting of a nonprofit organization and heard the leader of the organization say, "Our children are our gift to the future." What a profound statement! Think about the children you know. Are you preparing them for the future? How will you help them so they can make a difference? I recommend you lead by example and work to make a difference today.

Making a Difference

Libraries are great resources in our communities. When was the last time you visited your library? Do you have and use your library card? In these tough economic times, libraries can be wonderful places to find amazing books to read, music CDs to hear, DVDs to watch and outstanding programs in which to participate. Libraries make a difference in our communities...visit one today!

Making a Difference

Sitting in an airport, I began talking to a fellow traveler named Shaun who was also finishing up a business trip. Upon seeing the two books I was reading he shared his wife is an avid reader. He went on to say that they decided the books were overtaking their living space as they were stacked everywhere, even in the garage! Shaun informed me that they decided to donate the books that had been read to their local library! What an easy and wonderful way to make a difference!

Making a Difference

I read the book, Switch: How to Change When Things when Change is Hard, which you might imagine by the title, is about how to change things when change is hard. One of the stories shared as an example to illustrate this point is amazing. Most of us have never heard of Professor Jay Winston, but we have heard the term "designated driver". Do you recall how this term came into your consciousness? It was due to Professor Winston's efforts! It seems on a trip to the Scandinavian countries in the 1980s he realized this (meaning using a designated driver) was already a practiced norm, however in the United States it did not exist. So how in three years was he able to achieve success and change our way of thinking about drinking and driving? Professor Winston became very creative asking, collaborating and even cajoling at times producers, writers and actors of 160 prime time TV programs to add a "designated driver" moment in their plot lines. He didn't ask for large scenes or major discussions but for the words "designated driver" to be mentioned and/or used during a storyline. He was in essence asking for five seconds. By simply asking Jay Winston found a way to make a difference and what a difference it has made in all our lives!

Making a Difference

Have you heard of the Silk Road Theatre Project (silkroadproject.org)? I learned about it from my friend, Barbara, who is an actress and performed in a production. The Silk Road Theatre Project is a nonprofit organization showcasing playwrights of Asian, Middle Eastern and Mediterranean heritage and backgrounds. These playwrights and their works address and feature themes relevant to the peoples of the Silk Road and their Diaspora communities. Using the mediums of theater, video, education and advocacy, they present these works to Americans. In one of their efforts, seven women playwrights came together to create the documentary play "Seven" which tells the story of seven women from seven countries including Afghanistan, Cambodia, Ireland, Guatemala, Nigeria, Pakistan and Russia and their survival, strength and leadership! If you have the opportunity, see the play "Seven"...it is intense and thought provoking. The Silk Road Theatre Project and its programs are making a difference!

Making a Difference

Imagine receiving an email message from an Army sergeant serving in Afghanistan asking you to donate a guitar. What would you do? Well that is exactly what happened to Robin A. Weber who owns a high-end guitar business in Nashville in July 2009. Robin responded immediately sending a guitar to the serviceman. She also created Guitars 4 Troops (guitars4troops.com) a nonprofit organization that to date has donated more than 130 guitars to active duty servicemen and women. She has also reached out to other guitar makers and music stores for donations of guitars and accessories such as strings, pitch pipes and lesson books. As Robin told *The Chronicle of Philanthropy* in an interview, "If they can have a guitar to help them escape or remind them of home, I want to do anything I can to make their life a little more bearable while they are over there." Robin A. Weber is truly making a difference!

Making a Difference

The Nature Conservancy has an ambitious program. They have a goal to plant a billion trees, one at a time, in the fight to end climate change. Check it out (plantabillion.org) and see how you with The Nature Conservancy can make a difference!

Making a Difference

Watching a program, I learned that 24 to 26 million people in the USA have diabetes and that one in four does not know they have it. Approximately three million have Type I diabetes more commonly known as juvenile diabetes. Get tested today especially if you are extremely thirsty and urinate often. What you learn will make a difference in your life!

Making a Difference

Country music artist Steve Azar and his wife, Gwen, founded the Steve Azar St. Cecilia Foundation in 2006 as a way for them to give back to communities and causes for which they care. They chose St. Cecilia for the name as she is the patron saint of musicians and composers. Thanks to Steve and Gwen for making a difference!

Making a Difference

Many of us wonder what we can do to help nonprofit organizations daily especially if the economy has battered our charitable budget! One thing to consider is adding a tagline to all your outgoing email messages about your favorite nonprofit organization, one that you really care about helping! Assuming you are not prohibited from doing this by your employer or that you have access to a personal email address, you could place information about a charity that means a lot to you in the signature block. Information such as the mission of the organization, details about their goals, history of the organization, the date and location of the annual gala, walkathon or next fundraiser, the website, etc. could be shared with those you communicate with on a daily, weekly and monthly basis. It is an amazing and inexpensive easy way to share with others your passion for a particular cause or issue. Think about how many emails you send every day then consider doing this. It is truly an easy and affordable way to make a difference!

Making a Difference

Actor, director and humanitarian

Sean Penn founded the J/P Haitian Relief Organization
(jphro.org) after the January 2010 devastating earthquake in
that country. The nonprofit organization's focus is to save
lives and rebuild communities through sustainable solutions.
It has provided temporary housing for 50,000 Haitians and
medical care to many more. Thanks to Sean Penn for leading an effort to change lives and make a difference!

Making a Difference

The YWCA was founded in 1858 in New York City. As it states on their website, "Throughout our history, the YWCA has been in the forefront of most major movements in the United States as a pioneer in race relations, labor union representation, and the empowerment of women." Today their tagline and mission is "Eliminating Racism, Empowering Women". Learn more today about how this 150 year old organization is still making a difference!

Making a Difference

For many of us high school seems like a distant memory. Do you attend your high school class reunions? If you do attend them, consider starting an effort (assuming it doesn't exist) to raise funds for your alma mater. Most public high schools are facing the same budget shortfalls that we see throughout the country and world. They often need financial help to insure that the students are afforded and offered opportunities. Talk to the principal or superintendent and find a way to make a difference!

Making a Difference

Growing up, I watched many of the famous movie musicals. The ones that caught my attention were the westerns, especially the ones that depicted barn raisings, quilting bees and the harvests. In thinking back over those musicals, what I become aware of is how they are all about neighbor helping neighbor. By coming together to help a fellow homesteader, farmer or rancher, people who were sometimes strangers were making a difference. These movies are a great example of philanthropy at work. What can you do today to make a difference for your neighbors?

Making a Difference

Most of us have heard of Gloria Steinem and Marlo Thomas, but did you know that in 1972 with Patricia Carbine and Letty Cottin Pogrebin they began the first women's fund in the United States. They called it the Ms. Foundation for Women (ms.women.org). It's hard to remember but this organization was created during the height of the feminist movement. Its purpose was to secure funding and other resources for organizations that were raising the voices of women and providing solutions in communities throughout the nation regardless of class or race. The work of the Ms. Foundation for Women is still viable. Thanks to Gloria, Marlo, Patricia and Letty for making a difference!

Making a Difference

Community foundations are an important asset to philanthropy! The first one was established in Cleveland in 1914 as a way for the counties of Cuyahoga, Lake and Geauga to come together and insure the needs of the community were met. The community foundation concept was the result of Frederick Harris Goff, a well-known banker with the Cleveland Trust Company, who wanted to create a dynamic organization that would be responsive. Today almost every community and/or geographic area has a community foundation. Check the one out in your community today. They do amazing work, know the needs of the community and make a difference!

Making a Difference

One person with an idea can change an entire town and region. That is what Tom Patterson did. He was a native of Stratford, Ontario, a town located in Canada that was suffering the effects of a depressed economy. Tom's idea was to revitalize the community by creating a theater festival dedicated to performing the plays of Shakespeare as the town shares the same name as the birthplace of William Shakespeare. While there were many naysayers and doubters in the beginning, the first production opened in 1953 under a large canvas tent on the Avon River with Sir Alec Guinness speaking the following words, "Now is the winter of our discontent..." The Festival now runs from April through November but year round there are activities to do. Tom Patterson proves one person with a vision and a passion can make a difference!

Making a Difference

The famed author Jane Austen said, "What is right to be cannot be done too soon." This is a very true statement! What do you see that needs to be done in your community that can't be done too soon? By tackling the issue, problem or exploring the opportunity you will be making a difference!

_____

_____

_____

_____

_____

_____

_____

_____

_____

_____

_____

_____

_____

_____

_____

_____

_____

_____

_____

Making a Difference

Most of us know of the famed painter and inventor Leonardo Da Vinci after all he painted the Mona Lisa! I love this quote that is attributed to him, "Life well spent is long." How true and if your life is dedicated to helping others its affect will be long. You and your efforts to live life well will make a difference!

_____

_____

_____

_____

_____

_____

_____

_____

_____

_____

_____

_____

_____

_____

_____

_____

_____

_____

_____

Making a Difference

Did you know that 22,000 children die each day throughout the world from preventable causes? The US Fund for UNICEF believes that number should be zero! The Fund was established to help children have access to clean water, health care, nutrition, education, protection, emergency relief, etc. in more than 150 countries. Find out more about how the US Fund for UNICEF (unicefusa.org) is working every day to make a difference!

_____

_____

_____

_____

_____

_____

_____

_____

_____

_____

_____

_____

_____

_____

_____

_____

_____

_____

Making a Difference

Actor, director, writer, producer and Academy Award Winner Ben Affleck has used his celebrity status to raise awareness about issues he is passionate about including hunger in America, the escalating humanitarian crisis in the Congo and to address Congress about genetic disorders. Ben Affleck always finds a way to make a difference!

Making a Difference

Did you know that Andrew Carnegie is credited with ushering in the modern philanthropy era? In June 1911, he was granted a charter to create the Carnegie Foundation which was one of the first general purpose American foundations. Soon after John D. Rockefeller created his foundation and the "Modern Golden Age of Philanthropy" was off and running. Today it is estimated that there are 75,000 foundations in the USA and half of them were established in the last twenty years. One hundred years later and people are still wanting and working to make a difference!

Making a Difference

At the turn of the 20th century, philanthropy was viewed as charity or a hand out. The modern era of philanthropy is viewed as a hand up meaning it attempts to solve the causes of a problem, not just the symptoms. Practice your personal form of philanthropy today. You can be assured you will be making a difference!

Making a Difference

Known as a businessman and philanthropist, John D. Rockefeller worked to make change happen. He is credited with funding innovations in medical research that eventually led to the hookworm and yellow fever being eradicated. John D. Rockefeller was an extraordinary businessman and philanthropist who made a difference!

Making a Difference

𝒟𝒾𝒹 𝓎𝑜𝓊 𝓀𝓃𝑜𝓌 most professional sports teams have a dedication to charitable activities in their communities? I have witnessed firsthand what the Chicago White Sox Charities does to give back in the Chicagoland area. Not only are most of the players committed to giving back to a charitable cause, but so is the overall organization. My friend, Christine, oversees and manages the ball team's philanthropic endeavors. Check out your favorite sports team and find out what they are doing to make a difference!

Making a Difference

TIP OF THE DAY

Sometimes it seems like our efforts to make things better in the charitable world have little effect on making change happen. Don't give up! Your work, efforts and donations do make a difference even when you can't see the change!

242

Making a Difference

Olympia Brown was known as an American suffragist and is regarded as the first woman to graduate from theology school to become a fully ordained and full time minister. She is credited with saying, "He who never sacrificed a present to a future good, or a personal to a general one, can speak of happiness only as the blind do of colors." What can you do today to help others in the future? How can you make a difference?

_____

_____

_____

_____

_____

_____

_____

_____

_____

_____

_____

_____

_____

_____

_____

_____

_____

Making a Difference

If you are of a certain age, you know Jerry Lewis either as an actor, comedian or the sidekick of Dean Martin. However for 50 years, Jerry Lewis has been the national champion for finding a cure for muscular dystrophy and related disorders. His primary method to increase awareness and raise money has been through a telethon held over Labor Day Weekend. When it began the telethon was televised for 21 ½ hours; in 2011 it will be on air six hours. Since Jerry Lewis started this telethon, he has raised more than $1 billion for research and help. In 2010, Jerry Lewis hosted his last telethon. Let's all take a moment this year to thank Jerry Lewis for all he did to make a difference!

Making a Difference

Donations to charity are one of the last things you can still deduct from your taxes on your return. Think about the fact that during the lifetime of most of us political donations have been eliminated as a deduction against taxes, credit card interest has been eliminated as has the interest payments made on your vehicle loan. But you can still deduct your contributions to charity and know that you are making a difference!

_____

_____

_____

_____

_____

_____

_____

_____

_____

_____

_____

_____

_____

_____

_____

_____

Making a Difference

I was walking with my friend David to a restaurant when he pointed out a bookstore in the neighborhood inquiring f I knew anything about it. I answered that I did not and he proceeded to tell me that the bookstore was named Open Books and in his opinion was one of the best non-profit organizations. It made me curious so I went to their website (open-books.org) and found the following statement, "Open Books is an award-winning nonprofit social venture that operates an extraordinary bookstore, provides community programs, and mobilizes passionate volunteers to promote literacy in Chicago and beyond." If you don't live in Chicago, check out its website. If you do live in Chicago, consider stopping by and shopping. Either way, by learning more about this nonprofit organization, you will be making a difference!

_____

_____

_____

_____

_____

_____

_____

_____

_____

_____

_____

Making a Difference

I love country music! I was listening to a program and the Zac Brown Band shared about their involvement with the effort "Letters for Lyrics" program. This is a program that combines the efforts of the Zac Brown Band, Dodge Ram Trucks, South Ground Records and Soldier's Angels. It works like this: you write a letter to a soldier stationed overseas; you then take that letter to a Dodge dealership or a Zac Brown Band concert, who will in turn give you a free compilation CD produced by South Ground Records that is not sold; and finally, Soldier's Angels will make sure the letters are delivered to US Troops. What a wonderful example of many individuals, organizations and companies working together to make a difference!

Making a Difference

Do you send thank you notes? One of the things I try to do every day is send a handwritten note to someone. It could be thanking them for something they did or congratulating them on something that happened. Daily there are a number of opportunities to send a note to someone. I often find an article that might be of interest to someone, clip it and send it to them with a small note. Sending notes is an easy way to tell someone that I am thinking about them. It is one way I like to make a difference!

Making a Difference

It seems there is a lot of talk about our environment these days. But for those of us at a certain age, we will remember when the talk was simply about picking up litter and putting it in its place. Many of us will recall the television commercial that featured a Native American man walking and seeing a lot of trash and litter on the ground. The TV commercial closed with a single tear rolling down the man's cheek. Think of what could happen if each one of us simply picked up a piece of garbage/litter/trash each day and put it in the trash receptacle. I try to do this daily. t is my little way of trying to make a difference.

_____

_____

_____

_____

_____

_____

_____

_____

_____

_____

_____

_____

_____

_____

Making a Difference

One day a week, try not to use your car at all nor ride in anyone else's car. Use public transportation, walk, ride your bike or find things to do around your home and neighborhood. You will be making a difference in so many ways!

Making a Difference

I learned about a unique fundraising effort from an experience an acquaintance had traveling back from a trip to Italy. She shared the flight attendants announced on the PA system that they were collecting leftover "Euros" for UNICEF. What a unique idea. How many of us have returned from Europe or other foreign countries with that country's currency in our pockets wondering what to do with it? UNICEF works throughout the world helping children in difficult situations. By donating "leftover" currency from our vacations and travels to UNICEF, we can know we are making a difference!

Making a Difference

𝓘 love asking thought provoking questions to stimulate conversations. I used to always ask the question, "Do you know how a cashew grows?" Most people don't know the answer to this seemingly simple question. The larger question is where does the food you consume on a daily basis come from? Many people believe we should go back to eating locally meaning consuming what is grown in our geographic area when it is ready to be eaten. By doing so, they contend we will lessen our carbon footprint as well as possibly be healthier (i.e., less allergies, food borne illnesses, etc.). Think about trying to eat local and what is in season for a month by visiting your local farmers market and using/consuming the food that is available for purchase there. You might be surprised at how easy it is to make a difference on so many levels!

Making a Difference

Do you struggle with the decision of what gift to purchase for a couple getting married? Instead of giving a gift to the couple who is getting married, why not consider making a charitable donation in their name? When Prince William married Catherine (Kate) Middleton in the spring of 2011, they asked that in lieu of gifts donations be made to charity. Within two months of their nuptials, more than $1.6 million had been donated and would be dispersed to their pre-determined favorite charities. William and Kate used their special day to direct funds to charities in Great Britain, Australia, Canada and New Zealand! Thanks to them for making a difference and leading by example.

Making a Difference

Each day find a way to celebrate and honor this world we live in! One idea to consider is taking your own coffee cup into your local coffee house. By doing this you will reduce the paper cups used and be making a difference plus on certain days, such as Earth Day, many coffee houses give free coffee to those using their own cups! This again proves that little things do make a difference!

Making a Difference

In 2010, Miller Brewing Company launched it "Give a Veteran Piece of the High Life" Program. For every High Life cap or tab dropped off to participating retailers or mailed in, Miller High Life donates ten cents toward High Life Experiences for returning veterans. Money raised goes toward paying soldiers' way into sporting events, concerts, outdoor adventures and the list goes on. Check it out (millerhighlife.com) and see how easy it is to make a difference!

Making a Difference

Have you ever heard of the Ravinia Festival? Located just north of Chicago, this nonprofit organization started in 1904 and is the oldest summer music festival in the US. You can sit in the amphitheater or on the lawn bringing a picnic, meeting friends and listening to great music! Check it out (ravinia.org) and learn about how many in the Chicago area enjoy summer and music. The Ravinia Festival makes a difference.

Making a Difference

Earl Nightingale, a US motivational writer and author, said, "The more intensely we feel about an idea or a goal, the more assuredly the idea, buried deep in our subconscious, will direct us along the path to its fulfillment." I love this statement and think it aligns perfectly with the work being done by so many in the philanthropic world. Many people who feel intensely about an idea or goal working weekly, if not daily, to change the world and make a difference!

Making a Difference

Most of us find funerals difficult both in terms of knowing what to say and what to do. I read the book *Leadership* which was authored by Rudy Giuliani after the 9/11 tragedy. In it he said that funerals are not optional. He worked to make sure he attended every funeral of a fallen NYPD and FDNY member. He showed up and sometimes that is all it takes to make a difference!

Survey after survey shows that only seven to nine percent of us have an estate plan which includes a donation to charity. We can do better. By being purposeful and including your favorite charitable causes and nonprofit organizations in your estate plan or will, you will be making a difference!

_____

_____

_____

_____

_____

_____

_____

_____

_____

_____

_____

_____

_____

_____

_____

_____

_____

_____

_____

Making a Difference

When you travel, are you adventurous? Do you try new things that are specific to the locale in which you are visiting? On your trip somewhere, do what the locals do in terms of eating what they eat, going to the local establishments and learning more about the area. One way in which to do that is by visiting the local historical museum or society. By doing this, you will be making a difference!

Making a Difference

Hispanic Heritage Month is celebrated every fall during the months of September and October. Take time this year to find out more about the largest growing population in our country. They have many traditions and ways of helping others that make a difference!

Making a Difference

Do you buy American? Many individuals focus buying things made in the USA. Become a conscious consumer and make choices that align with your values. By doing this you will be making a difference!

_____

_____

_____

_____

_____

_____

_____

_____

_____

_____

_____

_____

_____

_____

_____

_____

_____

_____

_____

_____

_____

_____

Recycling seems to be on everyone's mind these days. But instead of only thinking about your garbage and trash think about your clothing. Consider having a "party" with your friends and each of you share the things you don't wear and/or want anymore. You might be surprised how easy it is to "spruce" up your wardrobe and to make a difference!

Making a Difference

If you serve on a Board of Directors for a non-profit organization, it is really important to pay attention. Too often, I have seen individual Board Members not read the minutes or look at the agenda until the day of the meeting, usually a few hours before. Serving on a Board of Directors is serious business as they are often viewed as the "head" or leadership of the nonprofit organization. Someone once told me that fish rots from the head and so do nonprofit organizations when Board Members don't pay attention. Do your part to be a good Board Member. You will be making a difference!

Making a Difference

Learn a new word every day. If you can't do it every day, try once a week. Find a way to use it in a sentence or conversation. By doing this you will not only be expanding your vocabulary but also making a difference!

Making a Difference

Kids still set up lemonade stands in the summer. When you see one, stop and purchase a glass or two of the refreshment. This simple act could inspire a budding entrepreneur on to greatness or be a way to support whatever cause for which they might be raising money. Two things are for certain: your thirst will be quenched and you will be making a difference!

TIP OF THE DAY

First Lady Michelle Obama started the Let's Move Campaign (letsmove.gov) which is an effort to fight childhood obesity. Commit and find a way to move every single day. By doing this you will be leading by example, becoming healthier and making a difference!

Making a Difference

Don't text and drive! The statistics are startling and the pictures are horrific of those who have been killed or severely injured as a result of texting while driving or being hit by someone who was doing this. Do your part to make the roads safe! Try to not text while driving for one day, then the next, then the next....you will be making a difference!

Making a Difference

Actor Don Cheadle co-wrote a book titled *Not On Our Watch* which depicts the Darfur crisis. It was his hope that the book would educate the public about a crisis. After the book was published, he co-founded a nonprofit organization with the same name with his *Ocean's Thirteen* co-stars including George Clooney, Matt Damon, Brad Pitt and others. Don Cheadle works to create awareness of the mass atrocities being committed as well as engaging others in the issue. He definitely is making a difference!

Making a Difference

When meeting with someone, give them your full attention. If you are in your office, do not check your emails or answer your phone unless you tell them you are expecting an email or call. By doing this, you will be fully engaged in the discussion and making a difference!

Making a Difference

Book clubs are a popular way of being committed to reading. If you are part of a book club, consider having a theme or topic to study for a year. It could be a time period, a geographic area or a group of people (i.e., the Civil War, the Civil Rights Movement, westerns, international authors, local authors, etc.). By becoming purposeful about the books selected you will be making a difference!

Making a Difference

When invited to someone's house for dinner, be a good guest. Eat what is served but be sure to share if you have a food allergy or an aversion to certain foods beforehand. Hosts usually work hard to prepare a special meal for their guests and by eating heartily while complimenting the cook, you will be making a difference!

Making a Difference

Did you know suicide is the third leading cause of death among teenagers? We must do better! Take time to talk to teenagers in your life, listen to them and monitor their social media activity especially for signs of bullying which some say are leading many to consider suicide. Do what you can to become aware and tackle this issue directly. Your knowledge and involvement will make a difference!

Making a Difference

Treetops Golf Resort located in Gaylord, Michigan started a program called, "Philanthropic Tuesdays". It allows a golfer to play for a cause on Tuesdays. If they golf nine holes, Treetops donates $5 to any nonprofit organization; if the person plays ten holes of golf, they donate $10 and so on. In 2010 Treetops Golf Resort donated over $55,000 to charity! They are committed to do more! What a unique and creative way to make a difference!

Making a Difference

𝒜𝓈𝓀 𝓆𝓊𝑒𝓈𝓉𝒾𝑜𝓃𝓈 before making financial donations! Most of us have heard the allegations of fraudulent actions about the nonprofit, Central Asia Institute and the *Three Cups of Tea* author Greg Mortenson. Whether they are true or not, it is an important example of the need for those of us who donate to ask basic and sometimes tough questions. There are organizations that can help you check nonprofits including the Better Business Bureau's Wise Giving Alliance (give.org). Be a smart donor; ask questions! You will be making a difference!

_____

_____

_____

_____

_____

_____

_____

_____

_____

_____

_____

_____

_____

_____

_____

_____

Making a Difference

Electric power plants are the largest industrial source of global warming. However, there are things you can do to reduce these pollutants. Experts recommend setting your thermostat in the winter to 68 degrees or less. Some even suggest setting the temperature to 55 degrees when you are away for the day. If you are cold, grab a sweater or warmer clothing and when sleeping add an extra blanket. Let the sun shine into your house in the winter, too. By doing this, you will be making a difference!

Making a Difference

Many of us are animal lovers and want to be sure they are free from fleas and ticks. However, did you know that many flea and tick collars have hazardous chemicals! Some of these chemicals have been linked to neurological problems such as learning disabilities in children and Parkinson's disease. Check out the safe options by going to the website (greenpaws.org). By doing this you will be making a difference!

Making a Difference

October is Domestic Violence Awareness Month. Annually domestic violence impacts millions of people in America. Statistics show that one in three women will experience domestic violence in their lifetime. More than ten million children are exposed to domestic violence in their homes every year. And it is estimated 3000 people lose their lives each year because of domestic violence. We must do better. We must work to eliminate domestic violence in our society. Take time today to learn the signs of someone being abused. It is the beginning of making a difference!!

Making a Difference

Drinking water is good for us. While many automatically reach for the plastic water bottle, I have learned that it takes twenty-six bottles of water to produce the plastic container for the one liter of water (or soda) and that the process pollutes twenty-five liters of groundwater! What are we doing? When I was growing up we drank water from the faucet or when playing outside, the garden hose. Why not return to the basics? You can purchase safe plastic or metal containers and begin using them for water. By doing so you will be making a difference!

Making a Difference

In 2009, twelve million barrels of oil were used to make the 88½ billion plastic bags used by shoppers in the United States. And surprisingly paper bags use four times more energy to make than plastic. The best choice to help the environment is reusable shopping bags that are made of cotton, nylon, etc. To insure you remember to use them, keep some of the bags in your car so that when you get out to go shopping they are in plain sight. By taking this easy step, you will be making a difference!

Making a Difference

Ever wonder what to do with your old cell phones, iPods, pagers, old cameras, etc.? The United State Postal Service began a "free" recycling program for small electronic devices. Simply go to the post office and put your old cell phone, iPod, pager, etc. in one of the free prepaid packages and it will be mailed to a center that either refurbishes or recycles these pieces of equipment. By doing this you won't be adding to the landfills and you definitely will be making a difference!

_____

_____

_____

_____

_____

_____

_____

_____

_____

_____

_____

_____

_____

_____

_____

_____

_____

Making a Difference

Many households receive numerous catalogs. Do you wonder how to stop the flow? There is help. You can go to a website (catalogchoice.org) and sign up to have the catalogs stop coming to your house. They should stop within ten weeks. By doing this you will reduce pollution, reduce paper filling the landfills and have an emptier mailbox. You will be making a difference!

_____

_____

_____

_____

_____

_____

_____

_____

_____

_____

_____

_____

_____

_____

_____

_____

_____

Making a Difference

Have you ever heard of the National Resources Defense Council (nrdc.org)? Founded in 1970, their mission is to safeguard the Earth, its people, plants, animals and natural systems. The website has numerous tips and ideas for individuals and families, many which are easily implemented. Begin accessing information from this nonprofit to explore how you can make a difference!

Making a Difference

Do you know the name Harvey R. Ball? He was hired in 1963 by State Mutual Life Assurance Company to create a design to boost the morale of employees. The key was that it had to fit on a button. Harvey R. Ball designed s simple yellow face with a smile that is easily recognizable today. He never copyrighted his design and within seven years it became public property. The smiley face that is easily recognizable throughout the world is the result of one man's idea. He was paid only $45 for his efforts but in a 2001 interview he said, "It's an amazing piece of art. It is understood by everybody. You can be a little kid...you can be elderly. Everybody knows smiley." Thanks to Harvey R. Ball for his generosity and for making a difference!

Making a Difference

The film *The Economics of Happiness* is about localization versus globalization questioning if globalization is a good thing for people and the Earth. It suggests that going back to a local focus (meaning communities being dependent and responsible for themselves) is the way to happiness. Check it out (theeconomicsofhappiness.org); by learning more about this topic you could make a difference!

_____

_____

_____

_____

_____

_____

_____

_____

_____

_____

_____

_____

_____

_____

_____

_____

_____

Making a Difference

In my hometown of Alpena, Michigan, I attended the Besser Foundation Excellence in Education Awards Dinner. This is an annual event honoring the top five percent of students from my alma mater, Alpena High School. What an amazing group of young people who all have hopes and dreams to change the world! Celebrate and support the hopes and dreams of young people in your community. They definitely will be making a difference!

_____

_____

_____

_____

_____

_____

_____

_____

_____

_____

_____

_____

_____

_____

_____

_____

_____

_____

Rainer Maria Rilke, a Bohemian-Austrian poet who is considered one of the most significant poets in the German language, said, "Perhaps everything terrible is in its deepest being something helpless that wants help from us." What if we were to live by this statement? It would make a difference!

_____

_____

_____

_____

_____

_____

_____

_____

_____

_____

_____

_____

_____

_____

_____

_____

_____

_____

_____

Making a Difference

American philosopher and psychologist William James said, "The greatest use of life is to spend it for something that outlives it." What a profound statement! What could you do today that would outlive you? I highly recommend trying to do at least one thing this day that would have long lasting effects and ultimately make a difference.

Making a Difference

The German poet, playwright and theater director Bertolt Brecht once said, "Don't be afraid of death so much as an inadequate life." What could you do today to have an adequate if not outstanding life? In other words, what could you do today in your life to make a difference to others?

_____

_____

_____

_____

_____

_____

_____

_____

_____

_____

_____

_____

_____

_____

_____

_____

_____

_____

_____

_____

Making a Difference

I love this quote by Helen Keller. It is reported she said, "When one door of happiness closes, another opens; but often we look so long at the closed door that we do not see the one which has been opened for us." This is true with your efforts to change the world. Don't keep looking at what didn't work; find a new way to make a difference!

_____

_____

_____

_____

_____

_____

_____

_____

_____

_____

_____

_____

_____

_____

_____

_____

_____

Making a Difference

American poet Wallace Stevens once said, "It matters immensely. The slightest sound matters. The most momentary rhythm matters. You can do as you please, yet everything matters." What you do today matters! Do something to make a difference!

TIP OF THE DAY

Charles Kingsley, a priest of the Church of England, professor, historian and novelist, said, "We act as though comfort and luxury were the chief requirements of life, when all that we need to make us really happy is something to be enthusiastic about." What are you enthusiastic about and how can you use your enthusiasm to make a difference today?

_____

_____

_____

_____

_____

_____

_____

_____

_____

_____

_____

_____

_____

_____

_____

_____

_____

_____

Making a Difference

You can hear amazing stories on the public radio. A story I heard detailed the efforts of one person making a difference. It seems Valerie Mann, a sculptor and painter in Michigan, was wondering what she could do to help others in the area who were struggling in this tough economy. She came up with an idea and then bounced it off her friend, Peter Bowe, who owned the Saline Picture Frame Company. The idea was to approach the artists they knew in the area to donate a piece of art, a sketch or something they could do relatively quickly. Then they would be framed and the art displayed in Peter's store. In seven years they have raised $100,000 for Food Gatherers, a nonprofit organization providing food to people in Washtenaw County located in southern Michigan. This year, there is a new twist to this model. The paintings and artwork of children will also be showcased and sold to raise money for Food Gatherers! What a unique idea and way to engage all aspects of the community in raising funds for those in need. Valerie and Peter definitely started something that is still making a difference!

Making a Difference

The Library of Congress was established in 1800 by President John Adams. The original purpose was to provide the Congress reference materials for their work. The Library was housed in the US Capitol until the British invaded and destroyed it in 1814. Within a month of its destruction, former President Thomas Jefferson offered to donate his personal library to the United States, which he had been amassing for 50 years, and it was accepted. Today, the Library of Congress is a national institution and treasure and you can make a donation just like Thomas Jefferson. Visit the Library's website (loc.gov) and consider making a donation. You will be making a difference, just like Thomas Jefferson did all those years ago!

Making a Difference

Lots of people tell me they think the ability to deduct donations to nonprofit organizations is the number one reason individuals make contributions. However, survey after survey reports indicates that this is not as important as perceived. How important is tax deductibility of a donation to you? Does it affect your giving habits? Would you stop giving if it were eliminated or would you continue to make a difference?

Making a Difference

Annually, set a charitable budget of how much you want to give away in terms of financial donations. Then determine the charities/nonprofit organizations that you care about most deciding how much you want to give to each. An extra tip is to set some additional dollars aside for those unexpected charitable requests. By following these recommendations you will be more purposeful in your charitable deductions and make a difference!

Making a Difference

My friend, Missy Lavender, started the nonprofit organization, The Women's Health Foundation. This organization is dedicated to women's pelvic health which is an often overlooked area of female health. As their mission states, "Women's Health Foundation strives to improve pelvic health and wellness of all women and girls." Check it out (womenshealthfoundation.org) and see how one woman is educating and improving women's health on a daily basis. Thanks to Missy Lavender for making a difference!

Philosopher Rajneesh said, "The moment a child is born, the mother is also born. She never existed before. The woman existed, but the mother, never. A mother is something absolutely new." What a profound statement about women and the role they play as mothers in making a difference!

Making a Difference

Anna Chan is a remarkable woman. In driving around her neighborhood located outside of San Francisco, she noticed lemons, oranges and apricots rotting in her neighbors' yards. It brought back memories of when she and her sister were being raised by a single mom and often were hungry. She recalled that most meals came out of can and that fresh fruit was a luxury. Upon seeing the rotting fruit, she vowed to do something about it. Since then, Anna, who is locally known as the Lemon Lady, has organized volunteers and harvested 250 tons of fruits and vegetables valued at $600,000. She picks up food at all hours of the day and drops it off at food banks. Anna Chan by seeing an opportunity, and recalling a time in her childhood when she was hungry, is definitely making a difference

Making a Difference

$\mathcal{D}o$ you $\mathcal{k}now$ the name Harmon Killebrew? He was a farm boy from Idaho that a US Senator thought might be an outstanding baseball player. The US Senator told the owner of the Washington Senators about his skill and ability and he was recruited. When the Washington Senators moved to Minnesota and the team was renamed the Minnesota Twins, Harmon embraced his new home in many ways including philanthropically. One of the things he did was to raise funds for the Miracle League, an organization giving disabled children a chance to play baseball. Harmon Killebrew, whose nickname was Killer, was anything but and worked to make a difference!

Making a Difference

While many of us think about our Thanksgiving celebration in terms of family gatherings and watching how much we will eat, hunger is a daily issue for more than 50 million Americans - many of them children and senior citizens. Consider what you can do to make a difference and insure those in your life and neighborhood are fed. Contact your local food bank or pantry to find out what you can do to make a difference!

Making a Difference

Casa Central is the largest nonprofit organization located in Chicago, Illinois primarily serving the Hispanic community. They feed more than 1000 children, youth and seniors as well as house and train seventy homeless families so they can rebuild their lives and become self-sufficient. Additionally, Casa Central cares for over 1500 senior citizens insuring they stay active and involved in their community. The work they do is amazing! Check them out (casacentral. org) and see how one nonprofit organization founded more than fifty years ago in Chicago continues to make a difference to many people!

Making a Difference

Music and dance play a big part in many of our lives. Have you been somewhere and simply wanted to break into song or dance? Well, you might have a chance. The Random Acts of Culture is a program of the John S. and James I. Knight Foundation to raise awareness and revamp support of the arts. Since October 2010, seemingly impromptu opera, dance, classical music, jazz and poetry performances have occurred in several cities around the US in airports, department stores, farmers markets, libraries, malls and a children's museum. By 2011, more than 250 Random Acts had taken place surprising many! The goal is to achieve one thousand Random Acts of Culture by December 2013. What a wonderful way to make a difference on so many levels!

Making a Difference

Scholarships are important and come in many different forms. Think about how you could commit to providing a scholarship for a student. It could be an academic scholarship at a high school or college/university or funding for a child to go to summer camp. The scholarship could cover costs of a field trip or a membership fee. There are many things you could support with a few dollars. Consider establishing a scholarship for a program that is important to you. You will be making a difference!

Making a Difference

Halloween is a special day to many children! What could you do to make this holiday extra special for a child? Could you help them with their costume? Make sure you have their favorite treats when they knock on your door? Plan a party? Begin planning now to do something special to celebrate a much loved holiday - your actions just might make a difference!

Making a Difference

On November 9 and 10, 1938,

Kristallnacht began throughout Germany and Austria. The Nazis terrorized people of the Jewish faith burning and destroying their homes, businesses and places of worship. But there are examples of people who took a stand and made a difference. Take time today to learn about these ordinary people who did extraordinary things during the Holocaust to make a difference!

Making a Difference

Veteran's Day is a time to remember those who have served and fought for America. Do something to honor this special day. Thank a veteran, make a donation to nonprofits serving veterans such as the Wounded Warrior Project, USO, Disabled American Veterans, etc. or take a moment to reflect on how lucky we are to live in this USA. There are so many ways you can make a difference!

Making a Difference

If you are like me and most people today, you are always in a hurry and often that leads to not paying attention to what is going on around you. Take an extra moment today and pay attention to the pedestrians and bicyclists that are sharing the road with you. In most municipalities, you are expected to yield to pedestrians and bicyclists. Do this one simple thing and you will be making a difference!

Making a Difference

When you travel, do you ever think about adding a volunteer component? It is a great way to give back to an area that you are visiting. Often we are so busy sightseeing and doing that we forget there are always needs in all communities. Consider finding a program or nonprofit organization with which to volunteer on your next trip or vacation. You will be making a difference!

Making a Difference

American born motivational speaker and author Jack Canfield said, "Procrastination is a way of protecting yourself from all the things you're afraid might happen. The cure to procrastination is action." What are you procrastinating on that would make a difference in your community if only you took action!

_____

_____

_____

_____

_____

_____

_____

_____

_____

_____

_____

_____

_____

_____

_____

_____

_____

_____

Making a Difference

If you are like most people, you receive many appeals each month asking you to make a charitable donation. Consider this strategy for sorting through all those requests received in the mail: simply collect all appeals received for a month, then once a month review them deciding to which you want to give a charitable donation. This is a way to be strategic while making a difference!

Making a Difference

How often are you asked verbally for a charitable donation? How do you respond? My recommendation is to ask for all verbal requests to be put in writing, especially those received over the phone. By doing this you will minimize your exposure to fraudulent appeals and be assured that the ones you are considering are legitimate. By making this simple request, that the appeals be in writing, you will be making a difference!

Making a Difference

Legal aid clinics do important work in many communities. They provide legal services to the poorest of the poor. Legal aid clinics often depend heavily on volunteers, especially attorneys who can review and take on cases to help them fulfill their mission. Check out the legal aid clinic in your community and see if you can find a way to help. You will be making a difference!

Making a Difference

My friends, Valerie and Greg, have two young sons. Annually, the family takes trips to various parts of the United States. In preparing for a trip to Washington, DC, they developed a strategy to help make the travel more fun for each of their boys. They shared with them the destination and asked each to pick a monument to study. One picked the Lincoln Memorial and one picked the Washington Monument. For the months leading up to the trip, each boy read books and studied about not only the Memorial and the Monument but also the men for whom they were dedicated. When the trip happened, each boy was the "expert" on his chosen tourist location. What a wonderful way to involve everyone in planning the trip and a great way to make a difference while taking a vacation!

Making a Difference

Do you find jewelry in your jewelry box that you have not worn in years? I recommend you consider giving these little worn pieces away to your nieces and other girls or women in your life. By doing this, you will see your jewelry worn again and be making a difference!

Making a Difference

Do you give gifts unexpectedly? I often find those are the best presents to give. A few years ago my youngest niece, Caitlin, wanted an American Girl Doll but knew they were really expensive. At a charity benefit, I won one and immediately called her mom, my sister-in-law, to ask when it should be given to her as both Easter and her birthday were coming up shortly. Her mom thought that perhaps we should wait because it would be an important gift in Caitlin's life. However, I decided that my niece needed to know that you can receive presents anytime. I sent the unexpected gift to my niece and she loved it! It taught her the lesson to give gifts anytime and it definitely made a memorable difference!

Making a Difference

Unexpected gifts are often the best if done spontaneously. For example pay the parking meter for the cars on the street as you pass by, especially those that have expired, buy the cup of coffee for the person in line behind you at the coffee shop, pay for the dry cleaning of the person next in line, etc. By doing things like these, you will be making a difference!

Making a Difference

All of us have many memories from our childhood. One of the ones I remember vividly is President Jimmy Carter in a blue sweater standing beside a thermostat in the White House. This was during the oil crisis in the 1970s and he was asking Americans to turn down their thermostats in an effort to decrease the United States' dependence on foreign oil. President Carter was demonstrating how one simple act, in this case turning down the thermostats in our homes, could make a difference!

Making a Difference

Experts say by leaving things on and/or plugged into outlets we are wasting energy. It is estimated that if we simply unplug our phone chargers, shut off our computers and printers when they are not in use or at night, we would be reducing our carbon footprint significantly. Check out your home and office. Are there appliances and equipment that are not used daily and could be unplugged? What a simple way to make a difference!

Presidents of the United States

make a difference everyday with their decisions and actions. Sometimes their decisions and actions are applauded and sometimes they are not. Each presidency has a story to tell and many of them are told through their Presidential Libraries. Why not include a trip to a Presidential Library for your next vacation? Considered a modern development Presidential Libraries are a wonderful opportunity to learn how both Democratic and Republican leaders worked to make a difference!

Making a Difference

I love stories! Often times we miss the very best stories because we do not ask for them to be told. When gathering with family members at various holidays and occasions, take time to ask for the elders to tell the family stories. Often you will find many unsung heroes who on a daily basis did something to make a difference!

Making a Difference

Have you ever considered a career in fundraising? There are many causes and nonprofit organizations looking for help and in need of individuals who can raise money. There are educational programs and even degrees that can now be obtained. Check out the nonprofit sector, and specifically the fundraising field, as a career choice or recommend it to those looking for career advice. Working daily in the nonprofit sector is a wonderful way to make a difference!

Making a Difference

Grammy Award winning musician Bono is almost as well known for his philanthropic efforts as for his music (and lyrics he writes for U2). He works to raise money to fight global poverty. Most of us are aware of his One Campaign and (RED). He has been often cited as the "the face of fusion philanthropy" by his successful efforts in bringing diverse leaders from all spectrums of life together including religion, government, philanthropy, media and business. He works tirelessly with world leaders advocating for third world debt forgiveness and raising awareness of the plight of Africa. One man who is constantly using his celebrity status and voice to raise issues that most of us don't think about on a daily basis. One man working to make a difference!

Making a Difference

Thomas Hampson is considered a great American lyric baritone. He founded the Hampsong Foundation, which is dedicated to supporting the art of song in America and around the world as a way to foster communication and understanding between cultures. The Song of America is the Foundation's current project which s being done in collaboration with the Library of Congress. Check it out (hampsong.org) and see how Thomas Hampson is working to everyday to make a difference!

_____
_____
_____
_____
_____
_____
_____
_____
_____
_____
_____
_____
_____
_____
_____
_____
_____
_____

Making a Difference

Have you ever heard of the disease Focal Dystonia? My friend and outstanding guitarist Billy McLaughlin (billymclaughlin.com) contracted this disease which affects a muscle or group of muscles in a part of the body and causes involuntary muscular contraction or twisting. For Billy, it affected his right hand. The film, *Changing Keys*, depicts his journey through discovery and recovery. Check it out and see how one man's journey through this disease has inspired many. Through his music and his recovery, Billy McLaughlin is making a difference!

Making a Difference

I love books! I often loan the ones I have read to people encouraging them to enjoy the look and feel! While many people are using e-readers now, I believe there is still value in a book. When was the last time you read a book? Would you consider loaning your books to others or donating them to your local library, domestic violence shelter, nursery school, senior center, etc.? By doing any one of these things, you will be making a difference!

Making a Difference

Another way to conserve our natural resources is to turn off the water when you are brushing your teeth. It is estimated that up to eight gallons of water is wasted when you let the water run while brushing. Take time to turn off the faucet; you will be making a difference!

Making a Difference

We often hear about how many hours of television watching is done by the average American. I challenge you to shut off the television for a week and do family activities such as playing games, talking or reading. By doing this, you will be making a difference!

Making a Difference

It is widely agreed that Country Music Artist Brad Paisley is an amazing guitarist and musician! But what is little known is his philanthropic spirit. When tornadoes devastated parts of Alabama in 2011, Brad decided to donate all the artist royalties from the US digital sales of "Old Alabama" to tornado relief through the American Red Cross. In 2010, when Nashville was ravaged by flooding waters, Brad took a visible leadership role even though all of his equipment was destroyed and he was preparing for a major new tour ironically called the H2O tour. He made it his mission to insure people were aware of what was happening and what was needed in terms of relief. Brad Paisley is always working to make a difference!

Making a Difference

World AIDS Day was started in 1988 to focus on increasing awareness, providing education, reducing incidence of prejudice and raising money. While AIDS is not in the headlines every day, it is important to remember that 33.3 million people are living with AIDS in the world and 2.5 million of them are children. Take time today to become educated and learn how you can make a difference!

Making a Difference

Have you heard about Soldier Ride, a program of the Wounded Warrior Project? It is a program that allows injured soldiers to ride adaptive bicycles by outfitting each bicycle to the specific rider. Soldier Ride is designed to build awareness and give hope that life goes on. But it also provides camaraderie for the numerous wounded military personnel who never thought they would be able to do something like this. Check it out (woundedwarriorproject.org) and see how one nonprofit organization is working daily to make a difference!

Making a Difference

The Twisted Pine Brewing Company, located in Boulder, Colorado, has a strong commitment to being involved in the community. Three years ago, the brewery decided to ratchet up its activities and contributions. According to owner Bob Baile they worked to get the employees and customers more involved. Each month the brewery has a program that benefits a different nonprofit organization. In the past groups such as the local Kiwanis Club, Autism Society of Boulder, KGNU public radio, the Colorado Therapeutic Riding Center and the local food pantry have received donations due to the efforts of the Brewery. Thanks to the Twisted Pine Brewing Company (twistedpinebrewing.com) for mixing business and doing good to make a difference!

Making a Difference

Locks of Love is a nonprofit organization that provides hairpieces to children under the age of 21 who are suffering from a medical long term hair loss and financially disadvantaged. As their website states, "Most of the children helped by Locks of Love have lost their hair due to a medical condition called alopecia areata, which has no known cause or cure. The prostheses we provide help to restore their self-esteem and their confidence, enabling them to face the world and their peers." Check out the website for guidelines on hair donations (locksoflove.org) and find out how you can help to make a difference!

Making a Difference

Most communities have historical societies or associations, some even have museums. Take time to check them out and learn more about your community. Historical societies, associations and museums often showcase those individuals who did something to change or enhance the community. Learn about those people who lived where you live and were able to make a difference!

_____

_____

_____

_____

_____

_____

_____

_____

_____

_____

_____

_____

_____

_____

_____

_____

_____

_____

_____

Making a Difference

When children become sick we hope and pray for a quick recovery. For most children this happens, however sometimes children have long term illnesses that require longer stays in the hospital. You can help. Think about becoming a volunteer in a pediatric ward. Often times there are programs for volunteers to play games and inter-act with the children who are ill. Contact your local hospital to see how you can make a difference!

_____

_____

_____

_____

_____

_____

_____

_____

_____

_____

_____

_____

_____

_____

_____

_____

_____

_____

Making a Difference

$\mathcal{D}o$ you $ever$ wonder what to do with those old games sitting around your house that you have not played in years? Consider donating them to a nonprofit organization that helps kids such as the Boys and Girls Clubs or to a school. Alternatively, if the games are appropriate for all ages, consider making a contribution to a nursing home or senior center. By doing this simple act you will be making a difference that will affect many individuals.

_____

_____

_____

_____

_____

_____

_____

_____

_____

_____

_____

_____

_____

_____

_____

_____

Making a Difference

Many of us forget that there are hungry people in our communities and neighborhoods. Hunger in America does not look like hunger in developing or third world countries. It could be the single mom down the street that skips a meal in order for her children to have food or perhaps the family that waters down the milk to make it go farther. These are realities that we often don't see. In order to remind you and your family that hunger exits, try sitting an empty plate and place setting at the table once a week to remind you that the issue of hunger still exists. You might also ask those who are at that meal to make a financial donation to the empty plate, then once a month take the donation to your local food bank or food pantry. By doing this, you will be educating those who dine at your table and making a difference to those that are hungry.

_____

_____

_____

_____

_____

_____

_____

_____

_____

Making a Difference

In tough economic times, people often stress about how to purchase gifts for special holidays such as birthdays, weddings, etc. Consider for one year giving only handmade gifts. Gift ideas could include baking a pie a month for someone, mowing someone's lawn for the summer, providing handmade coupons for babysitting or being the chef for an evening and providing a meal...the list of ideas could go on and on. By choosing to do something with your hands, the gift will be special and definitely make a difference!

Making a Difference

Do you shop at the thrift stores of nonprofit organizations? They are a great resource in our communities often filled with many treasures. Thrift stores are one of my favorite places to shop for unusual dishes such as serving platters, bowls, glasses as well as unique decorative items for the house. Next time you are in need of something, stop by your local thrift store as you just might be surprised at what treasures you find. By shopping at thrift stores you will be supporting the nonprofit organization and making a difference!

Making a Difference

Most of us have fond memories of the food from our childhood. We often find ourselves wishing we had the opportunity to taste those foods again, especially if trips home are infrequent or not possible. One of the best gifts my mom gave my sister, brother and me was an individual recipe box filled with her best and our favorite recipes. Now each of us has access to our favorite childhood foods anytime. What an amazing gift and a wonderful way to make a difference!

Making a Difference

Aldo Leopold was an American author, scientist, forester and ecologist. Early in his career, he was charged with hunting and killing bears, wolves, and mountain lions roaming in New Mexico. It seems that local ranchers hated these "predators" because of their livestock losses. But through time, Aldo learned to respect the animals. He eventually developed an ecological ethic that replaced the earlier wilderness ethic that had stressed the need for ultimate human dominance. Because of his willingness to change his mind and advocate for a different perspective, the result was the return of bears and mountain lions to New Mexico wilderness areas. By the 1930s, Leopold was the nation's expert on wildlife management. Learn more about his work by viewing the movie, *Green Fire: Aldo Leopold And A Land Ethic For Our Time*. See how one man by being willing to change his mind made a difference!

Making a Difference

Many of us have passed a street musician. Often times we don't even stop or pay attention. The next time you pass a person playing a musical instrument or perhaps an upside down five gallon plastic bucket, I encourage you to stop and spend a moment or perhaps a minute or two enjoying the music. You might be surprised how simply listening and giving a tip can make a difference!

Making a Difference

I read a story about a fellow Spartan alumnae! While attending Michigan State University, Jenn Gibson was a varsity rower. During her freshman year, she worked for a short time with a small group of women who were breast cancer survivors and rowers. Jenn had never known anyone who had breast cancer so this was a new experience and one that she never forgot. She realized that the women found healing in rowing together and putting their sights on getting to the finish line. When she moved to Chicago she was surprised to learn that no such group existed. So as you might suspect she started a team in 2008 with four rowers participating in the Recovery on Water (ROW). Today there are more than forty women between the ages of 30-65 that row three times a week. Research has shown that survivors who exercise regularly, meaning three to five times a week for at least thirty minutes, can reduce their chance of having cancer recur by fifty percent (50%). Jenn Gibson had an experience which she turned into a vision that ultimately led to making a difference for many women and their families!

_____

_____

_____

_____

_____

_____

_____

Making a Difference

I love birthdays and love celebrating them! When I am in a restaurant and it is someone's birthday at a different table, I always join in with the singing restaurant staff. It is a wonderfully easy way to make a difference to a complete stranger!

Making a Difference

Be willing to become a mentor. It is an important role you can play in a person's life. It is said that Laurence Oliver mentored Anthony Hopkins and Martin Landau mentored Jack Nicholson. It is even reported that Bach mentored Mozart! Mentors can have a profound impact on a mentee and definitely do make a difference!

Making a Difference

Breast cancer for women is a frightening diagnosis and disease. However, thanks to the Susan G. Komen for the Cure nonprofit great strides in research are being made. This foundation, like many others, came about because of a promise between sisters. In 1977 when Suzy was diagnosed at age 33 with breast cancer her sister Nancy was there as a rock of support. After three years and numerous surgeries, chemotherapy and radiation, Nancy made a promise to her sister that she would do something to help others battling this disease. The result s the Susan G. Komen for the Cure, a nonprofit organization that is the global breast cancer movement. Check it out (komen.org) and see how you can make a difference.

Making a Difference

Many people still love the movies! The culmination is the Academy Awards, usually held in February or March to celebrate all the best of the movies! Many people enjoy watching the television broadcast. This year, why not add a twist that will benefit a nonprofit organization? Consider hosting an Oscar party and have your attendees upon arrival complete a ballot form. To submit their ballot each person must contribute $5 (or perhaps $10 or $20) to participate. The person who has the most correct answers wins and gets to choose to which nonprofit organization the money contributed will be donated. What a fun way to make a difference!

Making a Difference

Many of us would like to do something meaningful to give back to our communities and neighborhoods. Consider becoming a docent. A docent is a tour guide or lecturer in a museum or other cultural institutions. Often these positions are voluntary and allow a person to work in an area of their interest (i.e., an art museum, historical society, architecture foundation, etc.) and to learn more. What a wonderful way to make a difference!

Making a Difference

Do you have a closet full of winter or other season coats you seldom, if ever, seem to wear? Consider donating them to a nonprofit organization that provides coats to those that need them. If you don't know where to begin to find such a group, ask at your local house of worship. They usually know where the need is the greatest and will direct you to the place where you can make a difference!

Making a Difference

I love art! One of the best gifts I received for a birthday was a handmade painting from each of my six nieces and nephews. Their moms had them paint or draw something for Aunt Lisa then framed all the pieces. Today, those six pieces of art hang on a wall outside my kitchen to remind me how the simplest things, such as paintings from a child, do make a difference!

Making a Difference

$\mathcal{O}$ne of the most unique ideas I became aware of was the Dispensary of Hope (dispensaryofhope.org). As their website states, "Millions of patients can't afford their prescriptions while billions of dollars of medications are wasted. Through innovative stewardship of the pharmaceutical supply-chain, we've built a national distribution center and pharmacy to support a network of dispensing sites and direct-to-patient prescription solutions." Their goal is to provide $50 million of medication to the uninsured by 2015. Check out this innovative idea and see how the Dispensary of Hope makes a difference!

Making a Difference

Does the flow of email you receive daily often seem overwhelming? Do you find misunderstandings and misinterpretations between staff members often have at their root an email? Several nonprofit organizations I know have declared one day a week, usually Fridays, "No Internal Email Day". This means that on Fridays, the staff cannot email one another but actually have to get up and walk to their colleagues' office/cubicle or call them and have a discussion. It is reported to have reduced the number of misunderstandings and definitely made a difference!

Making a Difference

We hear a lot about work/life balance but many of us have a hard time achieving this goal. Years ago, I read the book titled, *Margins* by Dr. Richard Swenson, in which he advocates for building in those time buffers or margins into our lives. One way to do this is to walk away from the cell phone, text and emails for a period of time. You could start by trying to do it one night a week or when you are on a vacation. By simply detaching from "electronics" you will be making a difference!

Making a Difference

For a long time, was always anxious around people with disabilities, believing I did not know what to do. I wondered should I offer to help push their wheelchair. lift a glass with a straw in it to their lips. etc. Then my stepfather, Uncle Don, had a leg and a foot amputated. It became obvious to me what I needed to do because this was a member of my family. I try to remember that when I see others who are disabled. I will often take the time to ask them if they need help crossing the street, getting onto a bus, etc. This is my little way of trying to make a difference!

Making a Difference

TIP OF THE DAY

Do you like to shop? Consider shopping via charity gift catalogs. By doing this you will accomplish two things: purchasing your gift and helping a charity. What a relatively easy way to make a difference!

Making a Difference

Most elementary schools have fundraising activities that include selling pizza, cookies and even wrapping paper. One of my favorite activities to attend is school carnivals. There is so much excitement by the children in their school, usually the gym, being transformed into a festive and fun atmosphere. If you get the chance, participate in a carnival. At any age, your participation will be fun, memorable to the child and help to make a difference!

Making a Difference

December is designated Drunk and Drugged Driving Prevention Month. The statistics are staggering but by following some simple tips you can be safer. The 1st is make a plan; the 2nd is become aware of potential challenging situations and the 3rd is if you are hosting a party, have options for your guests. By following these three simple tips, you will have a safer holiday season and be making a difference!

Making a Difference

Many of us know the song about the twelve days of Christmas. My suggestion is to take 12 days during the holiday season (or any time) to be purposeful about doing something each day to help someone else. Perhaps it's holding a door open for the person behind you, shoveling a neighbor's walkway, dropping some coins in a red kettle or buying a gift for a child that will not have a present! Do something each day for the next 12 days to make a difference!

Making a Difference

The American Red Cross facilitates a program to get holiday cards to US Troops serving oversees or recovering in stateside hospitals! The deadline is usually during the second week in December; cards must be addressed and postmarked by then to Holiday Mail for Heroes, PO Box 5456, Capitol Heights, MD 20791-5456. Make time today to mail a card to a soldier. You will definitely be making a difference!

Making a Difference

$\mathcal{D}o$ you $want$ to be a Santa Helper this year insuring every child has a gift under the tree? If yes, go to your local post office! For almost 100 years postal workers have been Santa Helpers insuring that the letters to the North Pole get answered. What is surprising is this year kids are asking for basic needs instead of toys (i.e., coats, socks, mittens). You can help and make a difference!

Making a Difference

The Salvation Army Red Kettles are out during the months of November and December. Many of my friends help out in their towns by ringing the bells to secure donations. If you are passing by, please consider putting money in the red kettle! The Salvation Army does amazing work year round and counts on us to come through during the holiday season. Yes, your donation will make a difference!

Making a Difference

The December holiday season can be stressful for many people with pressure to shop, send holiday cards, get the right gifts, etc. Why not start a new tradition with your family. The author Debbie Macomber and her family begin the holidays with an all night family slumber party! It began with the girls but now everyone has joined in making homemade gifts during the night. The Macombers are creating new and long lasting memories as well as making a difference to their family members!

_____

_____

_____

_____

_____

_____

_____

_____

_____

_____

_____

_____

_____

_____

_____

_____

Making a Difference

Many people wonder if there is a deadline for making a charitable donation. Contributions to nonprofit organizations can be made any time throughout the year! However, in order for your charitable donations to count as tax deductions for the year they must be made by 11:59 pm on December 31st. The postmark on the envelope must be marked by that time. If you are making a contribution via credit card, make it a few days prior to December 31st to allow time for processing. Do something now to make a difference!

Making a Difference

Many people wonder about what type of record keeping is necessary for charitable donations. Here are some tips: first, for donations over $250 you should automatically be receiving a receipt from the nonprofit organization. For any donations of clothing/furniture/equipment, the government is requiring additional detail for "used goods". Be sure your receipts have the date of the donation, value assigned, name of the receiving organization, condition of the donated product etc. Donating to charity, either in the form of money or products, is a way to be sure you are making a difference!

Making a Difference

I love this quote by Henry Drummond, an English banker, politician and writer, "You will find, as you look back on your life, that the moments that stand out are the moments when you have done things for others." Take time to make a difference in someone's life today!

Made in the USA
San Bernardino, CA
28 February 2015